LIVING IN TROUBLED TIMES

A New Political Era

Thierry de Montbrial

World Scientific

NEW JERSEY · LONDON · SINGAPORE · BEIJING · SHANGHAI · HONG KONG · TAIPEI · CHENNAI · TOKYO

Published by

World Scientific Publishing Co. Pte. Ltd.
5 Toh Tuck Link, Singapore 596224
USA office: 27 Warren Street, Suite 401-402, Hackensack, NJ 07601
UK office: 57 Shelton Street, Covent Garden, London WC2H 9HE

Library of Congress Cataloging-in-Publication Data
Names: Montbrial, Thierry de, author.
Title: Living in troubled times : a new political era / Thierry de Montbrial,
 French Institute of International Relations, France.
Other titles: Vivre le temps des troubles. English
Description: New Jersey : World Scientific, [2018] | Includes bibliographical references.
Identifiers: LCCN 2018034370| ISBN 9789813275874 (hardback) |
 ISBN 9789813276383 (pbk.)
Subjects: LCSH: International organization. | International relations. |
 Civilization, Modern--21st century.
Classification: LCC JZ1318 .M663613 2018 | DDC 327--dc23
LC record available at https://lccn.loc.gov/2018034370

British Library Cataloguing-in-Publication Data
A catalogue record for this book is available from the British Library.

This book is the translation of the French Edition *Vivre le temps de troubles*, Albin Michel, October 2017.

Copyright © 2019 by Thierry de Montbrial

All rights reserved.

For any available supplementary material, please visit
https://www.worldscientific.com/worldscibooks/10.1142/11147#t=suppl

Desk Editor: Daniele Lee

"I was confined to the present, as heroes are or drunkards; eclipsed for the moment, my past no longer projected before me that shadow of itself which we call our future."

Marcel Proust
Within a Budding Grove

Contents

Foreword ix

I. THE PRESENCE OF THE FUTURE

The Anthropocene: geology on a human scale 3
Energy: the natural agent of change 9
Information and artificial intelligence 15
Between reality and fiction 23
Looking beyond science fiction 27
Back to Earth 35

II. FOOTPRINTS FROM THE PAST

The usefulness of history 47
Scientific, technological and economic roots of the
    contemporary world 55
Modernity and progress 71
Back to religion 83

III. THE SHOCK OF THE PRESENT

Geopolitics and international politics 93
The primacy of the United States 101
Certainties and uncertainties regarding China's rise 105
The difficult governance of the global economy 109
The end of the Cold War: a missed opportunity 113
The European Union between peril and hope 119
The international system 129

Epilogue 143

Foreword

The idea for this essay started with my conviction that in the 1990s, the end of communism and the fall of the Russian Empire would not mean the much-heralded dawn of happy globalisation and everlasting peace. The current international system is tainted with the resurgence of old quarters. It is rendered increasingly complex by an unprecedented technological and economic revolution. Sustainable peace and prosperity can only be based on a shared understanding of the nature and effects of interdependence in every area — the bedrock of what is commonly called "global governance", which cannot be conceived in an ivory tower. Its emergence can only stem from continuous cooperation between international relations players, analysts and thinkers from the five continents.

Living in Troubled Times

Fostering that interaction is one of the main tasks of think tanks, a category of institutions that appeared in the 20th century.[1] Though it can be said that any initiative of this nature is just a drop in the ocean, the ocean needs every drop it can get.[2] To this end, in 2007, I set up the World Policy Conference,[3] a non-governmental organisation aiming to improve global governance by nurturing the viability of a world that is reasonably open, prosperous, and, therefore, fairer and more respectful of the diversity of states and nations. The problem is viability. As luck would have it, the first World Policy Conference took place in October 2008, several days after the collapse of Lehman Brothers, setting the stage for an economic meltdown comparable to the Great Depression. Moreover, peacekeeping in the post-Soviet world has proved challenging, especially in the Near and Middle East.

I mentioned that global governance cannot be conceived in an ivory tower. That touches upon an old philosophical question: the limits of knowledge without experience. I admire authors of treatises on the establishment of everlasting peace, such as the Abbé de Saint-Pierre and Immanuel Kant in former times or Jürgen Habermas today. Even law, to be effective, must

---

1 See "*Think tanks* à la française", an article co-written with Thomas Gomart, published in *Le Débat*, no. 181, September-October 2014, and "Qu'est-ce qu'un *think tank*?", a talk by the author at the Académie des sciences morales et politiques on 28 February 2011. Both texts were published in Thierry de Montbrial's *La pensée et l'action*, Academia Romȃna, 2015.
2 See Thierry de Montbrial, *Une goutte d'eau et l'océan*, Albin Michel, Paris, 2015.
3 See www.worldpolicyconference.com

be embodied. And the time when peace can be achieved and embodied in the law, has not yet arrived.

The goal of this book is at once both modest and far-reaching: to contribute to a better understanding of our times and to spur a wide-ranging debate on the state of the world today that is capable of reaching a consensus broad enough to better lay the groundwork for the future. I am aware that a perfect, lasting consensus is impossible outside moments of grace, such as the climate change agreement. But I think that it is realistic to hope for sufficient consensus to move forward on governance.

This essay begins with the notion that the present is the intersection of a future already here and a past not yet over. I shall start with the future, for the outlook has never seemed so exciting yet disturbing at once. Some upheavals are already underway in embryonic states. Others, more or less foreseeable, are yet to come. Much of what is expected will remain a matter of the imagination. There will certainly be completely new surprises. Mistakes are and will always be made in dating even the surest forecast. And let us keep in mind the human propensity to overestimate short-term changes and underestimate long-term transformations. Human beings are not the masters of time, but they are free to choose their own paths. That is especially true in terms of technological and economic development. In addition, change is not just radical. Contrary to popular belief, some topics, such as religion, belong as much to the future as to the past. There are also godless "religions":

communism, justified by dialectical and historical materialism yesterday and still somewhat today; as well as "singularity" and transhumanisation tomorrow and already today. As for the past, it is important to remain keenly aware of it. Anyway, it never fades from the unconscious. The usefulness of history, on which Paul Valéry meditated so well in difficult times — not just political history and the history of ideas, but also the history of science and technology — remains key. If it can be said that we are living in troubled times, it is largely because the breathtaking growth of knowledge in the 20th century has suddenly left us bereft of our traditional bearings. That accounts for why it is necessary not only to trace those developments, but also to re-examine the very idea of progress. A loss of bearings also means a loss of meaning. To find it again, distance is necessary for perspective. This applies to everything, including religion.

That said, the shock of the present results from the clash of two kinds of tectonic plates, past and future. I address the issue mainly from the geopolitical aspect, for that is the nature of the backdrop of governance. To make cooperation possible, however, the terms must first be defined. The concept of geopolitics is overused, which further convolutes discussion.

The only way to successfully weather troubled times is to personally and collectively try and make the best of the present. We are living in the most amazing epoch in world history. Hard as it may be to fathom the future, it must at least be assumed that humanity is not coming to an end. We owe it to future generations to work on building a framework, global by necessity, which will safeguard their chances of self-fulfilment. But we must also keep in mind that this will be neither quick nor easy. In this civilisation of instantaneousness, to advocate for the return of a long-term perspective, whether peering towards the future or back to the past, is not the least paradoxical.

I
THE PRESENCE OF THE FUTURE

The Anthropocene: geology on a human scale

Speaking at the Pontifical Academy of Social Sciences in February 2000, the winner of the 1995 Nobel Prize for chemistry, Paul Crutzen of the Netherlands, surprised his audience by proclaiming the dawn of a new geological era, which he called the Anthropocene. He even dated its inception to a specific year: 1784. The idea that mankind and the planet interact and contribute to shaping landscapes together is the basis of geography, the old academic discipline[1] that studies the face of the Earth. Crutzen was the first to assert that human activity could also affect the globe's most vertically extended movements in its atmosphere or, especially, in its bowels, where change is measured on a scale whose customary unit is one million years. Those are the movements

---

1 I am thinking, for example of Strabonius's *Geography*, written around 2,000 years ago. Les Belles Lettres published a bilingual French-Greek edition in 1969.

with which geology, the science of the history of the entire planet — especially its crust — is concerned.

Geological periods (or other units defined by chronostratography) are separated by major events, such as the opening of the seas or oceans or the formation of mountain ranges. In the Earth's history, those events signal times of rupture that typically mark the sometimes sudden transitions between the dynasties of ancient China or Egypt. Geology is inseparable from palaeontology, usually defined as the branch of science concerned with fossil animals and plants.

Saying that hundreds of millennia of life have left their mark on the Earth is therefore commonplace. What is uncommon is to assert that mankind is quickly — namely, in a matter of several generations — transforming not just the Earth's surface, but its very crust. Furthermore, it is exceptional to date the start of that phenomenon to a specific year! Geologists subdivide the most recent period, the Quaternary, into two epochs: the Pleistocene, which began around two million years ago, and the Holocene, which was slightly over 10,000 years ago — yesterday on the geological time scale.

Crutzen's boldness was to claim that mankind plays a key role in the Earth's immediate history, even beyond the thin film of soil, subsoil and atmosphere around it. It was to give a starting point — 1784 — with a precision that is normally meaningless in geology. That is the year James Watt patented his steam engine, which launched the Industrial Revolution and an unbroken string of technological changes that are not just ongoing to this day, but accelerating before our eyes. One could argue that, in material terms, the human condition as a whole changed very little from the dawn of recorded time until the late 18th century. Technological breakthroughs have continued apace since then. For a long time, they were rightfully considered the driving force of progress. Even before Watt's invention, Diderot's *Encyclopaedia*, the quintessential Enlightenment work, deemed the mechanical arts of vital importance. The progress of science and technology has brought about an unprecedented demographic revolution: the human population soared from 900 million in 1800 to 7.4 billion in 2016. That trend continues, accompanied by revolutionary changes in the patterns of human habitat, with a major shift towards cities and, especially, megacities.

It took two centuries, two world wars and several major economic and social upheavals for the wealthy countries, convinced that the end of world poverty was at hand, to start seriously worrying about the negative effects of what is now called growth. It is no coincidence that, in Europe, environmental movements appeared in early 1960s Germany, less than 20 years after the fall of Nazism. More recently, alter-globalisation movements emerged, identifying the negative aspects of growth with the unwanted effects of "liberal globalisation". The first United Nations Earth Summit took place in 1972 — the same year as the famous Club of Rome report *The Limits to Growth*, whose inspiration was prophetic but whose scientific foundations were wobbly, if not downright fanciful. The most impressive manifestation of industrial civilisation's negative effects on the "Earth system" is global warming, on which scientists have today reached nearly unanimous agreement — though this does not exclude the possibility that the phenomena observed could also have non-anthropic causes. The December 2015 Paris agreement on climate change is promising, although a truly coercive framework for States is obviously still a long way off. It could not have been otherwise, given the state of international relations today. The agreement will not end global warming and the increase of extreme meteorological phenomena, to which we must learn to adapt. It will still take many ordeals and a long global governance learning process before international cooperation bears clearly identifiable fruit in terms of prevention. In the short-term, Trump's election is a discouraging sign. We can expect other signs to follow.

Once again considering Crutzen's idea, climate change is the first indicator of the Anthropocene Era, which is accompanied by many other effects, such as the modification of the biogeochemical cycles of water, nitrogen, phosphate and phosphorus; shifts in erosion and sedimentation processes; changes in the oceans' oxygen content and, consequently, aquatic life; and the reduction of biodiversity. The list goes on. The increasingly spectacular effects on glacial masses have repercussions on volcanic and tectonic activities. It is not absurd to speak of a new geological era, surprising as that may seem at first. True, Crutzen is not a geologist but a geochemist, and the competent commission for defining the stratigraphic scale has not recognised his proposal. But the key point is that he sought to draw attention to the impacts of human activity that may have greater effects on the planet than those of which we had finally become aware of. He also suggests leads for research whose findings, like that of the IPCC[2], will gradually shed light on the paths to follow towards global governance in the decades and centuries to come.

---

[2] The Intergovernmental Panel on Climate Change (IPCC) is open to all UN member countries.

Energy: the natural agent of change

Men draw from nature the necessary resources to meet their own needs, which they define according to their current aspirations — which are not always reasonable, but that is a different story. To that end, they need two things: energy and information, the most basic production factors for economic activity.

Energy is the natural agent of change. Simply put, it is everything that can be converted into heat, the "lowest" form of energy. In theory and in practice, energy is inseparable from time. Until the Industrial Revolution, men mainly relied on muscle power: their own and that of the animals they domesticated. Naturally, animal power comes from the energy absorbed mainly as food and transformed by the metabolism process. Men gradually learned to use other natural forces (turning potential energy from gravity into kinetic energy, for example), first by multiplying the effects with phenomena such as the lever, then by using chemical energy in certain situations (heating with wood and, later, coal, biomass, etc.). Scientific advances based on those practical experiences allowed the "mechanical arts" to reach a high level of perfection as early as the Age of Enlightenment.

But the invention of the steam engine is what set the great technological revolution in motion, constantly rekindled by other, no less considerable discoveries, often associated with new forms of energy, including a wider range of fossil fuels (oil and natural gas), electricity, nuclear power, etc. Like financial assets, energy takes many imperfectly interchangeable forms. Entropy (i.e. the phenomenon by which all isolated systems evolve towards chaos) — a record of time passing — translates that imperfection, which makes heat the lowest form of energy. For example, animal power results from chemical processes set in motion by feeding them; and electricity can now be generated from the potential energy of water, wind, fossil fuels, atoms and sunlight. Power is hard to store, but swift progress is being made. Breakthroughs in battery technology have brought the reign of the electric car within reach, although arguably not nearly as soon as people may think.

The sun is the ultimate source of every form of energy available on Earth, but the physical processes at work radically diverge depending on how long their cycles are. Fossil fuels are solar energy stored on the scale of geological time. At the opposite end of the spectrum, 21st century solar panels instantly convert sunlight into electricity. Wind turbines, the descendants of windmills, generate power from the mechanical action of atmospheric movements, whose origins date back to the star we are revolving around.

The development of energy technology has kept pace with advances in physics. For example, it has been known since Einstein that, theoretically, energy and matter can be completely transformed into each other: the energy–matter tandem is a single reality. However, that assertion bears interpretation. According to the theory of special relativity ($E=mc^2$), the mass of a chocolate bar is equal to eight times more than the energy released by the explosion of an equal amount of TNT. But this surprising fact has no practical application. Chocolate is not an explosive and cannot be used in a nuclear power station! As for solar power, its economic exploitation is based on photovoltaic cells, whose physics obey the laws of quantum mechanics. Nuclear and solar power would have been unthinkable within the framework provided by classical physics prior to the 20th century.

At the basis of the Anthropocene Era, then, lies the prospect of a sort of human domestication of the sun. On a human time scale, our star seems like an endless source of energy. Yet, many unresolved challenges continue to impede the access and use of this energy. Hydroelectric power comes up against geographical limitations. Despite the progress of extraction technologies, fossil energy is not renewable on the human time scale and, worse still, its emission of carbon dioxide is disrupting the planet. Nuclear power is cleaner to begin with, but raises unresolved safety and security issues. Perhaps it will be impossible to eliminate or store radioactive waste. Lastly, wind turbines can mar the landscape and cause sound pollution.

Direct solar power looks more promising due to the applicability of Moore's law. Formulated in 1965 by the co-founder of the integrated circuit manufacturer Intel, Moore's law states that the number of transistors in a dense integrated circuit doubles approximately every two years. That also seems to apply to solar panels, which would help to make them less expensive and solve their main problem, namely the amount of ground space they occupy. Other technologies that seem to have a bright outlook, although not in the immediate future, include hydrogen-powered cars. Moreover, we should not lose sight of nuclear energy. In the long-term, the dream of nuclear fusion has still not yet vanished.

In his 2014 book *The Zero Marginal Cost Society*, futurologist Jeremy Rifkin heralded the imminent arrival of an age when limitless clean energy will be available at quasi zero marginal cost. The terminology used is important. The marginal cost of any given item is that of an additional unit of that item. As a general rule, production capacity is limited. Below peak capacity, the marginal cost can become very low, if not almost nil. Hereafter, new facilities and fixed costs are necessary. Rifkin's announcement sounds less groundbreaking when that key distinction is made. His idea of "imminent" is two decades. Power companies generally do not share his optimism, or at least disagree with the timeframe. What's more, technological research has a Darwinian aspect.

Energy: the natural agent of change

The most successful projects are not always the most expected ones. One thing is clear: the revolution continues, and it must be seized on the fly.

Information and artificial intelligence

If energy is the material agent of change, information is the key to decision-making. Energy, in the sense mentioned above, is a physical magnitude. Human beings, alongside their physical dimension, also have a psychic energy, which constitutes the basis of their creative capacity and, therefore, of their freedom. We must bear in mind that although technology may follow its own specific logic of development[1] — making certain forecasts possible in this area[2] — it remains the work of men. Information can also be understood as a physical value, as well as a psychic reality — intuition, for example.

---

1 See Kevin Kelly, What Technology Wants, Viking, New York, 2010.
2 On the notion of forecast in general, see "La prévision: sciences de la nature, technologie sciences morales et politiques" in Thierry de Montbrial, La pensée et l'action, Academia Romana, Bucarest, 2015, p. 685-739. An abridged version of this text can be found on the website of the Académie des Sciences morales et politiques.

In the broadest sense of the term, one could argue that information amounts to the degree of the decrease of uncertainty of an answer to a question one asks or might ask oneself. The degree of the decrease depends on collecting and processing data. If I toss a coin, I know ahead of time that, for reasons of symmetry, two answers are possible: two equally probable results. That situation corresponds to a unit of information (the degree of decrease between the uncertainty before and after tossing the coin — which is nil), called the bit. If I know beforehand that the coin is loaded, or that both sides are identical, the uncertainty of the outcome is zero. It is noteworthy that, for underlying reasons, a formula analogous to that which expresses entropy in statistical physics can measure an amount of information. In both cases, it is a matter of assessing a degree of disorder or, rather, of unknowingness.[3]

The relationship between information and energy can be shown from a different perspective because, in actual practice, the more information one has, the less expensive it is to reach one's goals. For example, a good traffic forecast allows drivers to save fuel. Likewise, weather forecasts cut the cost of air travel. Generally, on the economic level, the value of a piece of information (i.e. the reduction of uncertainty) for a user is equal to the amount of money it allows him to save in the pursuit of a goal. If the price of acquiring information is lower than the amount

---

3 See Ian Ford, Statistical Physics-An Entropic Approach, John Wiley & Sons, 2013.

saved, the beneficiary makes a profit. As for any commodity, it is useful to make a distinction between the producer's profit (the selling price minus the production cost) and the consumer's profit (the difference between the value he personally attributes to the item and its purchase price). A producer of information generally seeks to sell it to anybody who considers it valuable. Often, information is a collective good, in the sense that a more or less high number of people can fully and simultaneously use it. That is typically the case of traffic or weather information, which, in the current economic reality, are partially treated as public goods (free dissemination on television, radio and the Internet) or as private goods, accessible with a code and invoiced, such as weather reports for airlines. The structure of information markets is diverse by nature. Another example is in the area of private goods. If I have reason to believe that two gold ingots are buried somewhere in my backyard, I will not start looking for them if the cost of the search is sure to exceed their worth. But I would be willing to give one to somebody who knows exactly where they are buried and agrees to sell me that information. In that case, I would make a profit equal to the value of one ingot.

Rifkin argues that, just as for energy, the marginal cost of information tends towards zero — hence the title of his book. In fact, it refers to the marginal cost below a certain maximum capacity. But the meaning of such a prediction should be made clear in order to not confuse the cost of producing information (acquiring and processing data with a view to reducing the uncertainty of answers to well-asked questions) with that of transmitting it. The transmission cost can be almost nil and that of production or acquisition high, as it is still the case for weather forecasts.

The link between information and energy is most obvious in transmission technology, whether based on analogue signals, waves or coded series of bits. The bit, a unit of information, is a signal that can take two values in an equiprobable manner, symbolically 0 or 1. The first information revolution dates from the discovery of electricity, then Hertzian waves (Maxwell's equations) and electronics (semi-conductors), which led to the telephone, radio, television and computers. These were first designed as "electronic calculators" processing information with electronic circuits (which have become integrated circuits), whose functioning is isomorphic with binary logic operations. Their worth beyond digital calculation was quickly grasped, leading to the development of "information systems" meeting the needs of all kinds of organisations. Computers were being connected to each other in networks with increasingly advanced developments as early as the late 1960s, leading to the creation of the Internet. One of the most recent developments is cloud computing. It was just a matter of time before telephony, radio broadcasting, television and computers converged, providing a good example of predictability in the technological domain, and mobility increased (tablets, smartphones, etc.). While this trend continues to follow a partially predictable logic, computing power continues to develop at an increasingly low price both on the hardware and software side. Quantum computers are on the horizon, and engineers are ceaselessly developing increasingly ingenious algorithms such as those that made Facebook (social media), Google (search engines), Amazon, PayPal and many other companies successful. An algorithm is a series of ultimately binary instructions intended for a person or a machine to process data with a view to solving a problem step by step. Today, they allow billions of operations per second to be performed. Combining those advances cleared the way for big data processing, rendering the interconnection of devices possible (concept of *Internet of things*) and significantly broadening the prospects for artificial intelligence.

Artificial intelligence (AI) originated in the 1950s with the goal of achieving the age-old dream of building "thinking machines" capable of replacing, if not surpassing, humans in most of their activities.[4] It started with the now barely believable idea that it would be possible to devise a universal language adapted to every human need and, based on that language, to logically process every conceivable proposition in compliance with its rules. One of its first pioneers was Leibniz, who searched for such a language and made a "calculating machine" expanding on Pascal's ideas. But AI did not really enter — nor revolutionise — the realm of technology until 20th century "electronic calculators" emerged.

---

[4] See Marius Flasiński, *Introduction to Artificial Intelligence*, Springer, 2016; Jan Romportl et alii, *Beyond Artificial Intelligence*, Springer, 2015; Ian Goodfellow et alii, *Deep Learning*, The MIT Press, 2016.

It quickly became clear that combinatorial tasks considered the hardest by humans (such as chess or Go) are, in theory, the easiest for computers to execute. In 1997, IBM's Deep Blue robot beat the world chess champion, Garry Kasparov. On the other hand, the easiest tasks for humans (such as shape recognition) are harder for computers. Solving problems such as face or voice recognition is based on algorithmic methods and on the interaction between the machine and its environment that go beyond the execution of combinatorial tasks, so that the machine is capable of "learning" from that environment (deep learning). The success of these methods is undoubtedly the main characteristic of our contemporary world at the technological level.

The swift growth of artificial intelligence in all areas is the result of advances in a number of fields — not just computer or Internet technology, but also neurology, psychology, mathematics, linguistics and philosophy — which helped expand the reach of algorithms. However, the growth of artificial intelligence inevitably causes an increasing number of jobs to disappear. For example, the expected number of truck drivers to be affected when driverless vehicles become common in the United States is estimated to be at several million. Humanity is entering a new, dizzying, exciting but also frightening world where the line between dreams and reality is fading.

The remarks above make it easy to understand that the cost of transmitting and processing information may continue to plummet in the near future, still taking into account fixed costs. It also suggests that the same will be true for *producing* all forms of information in the more or less near future. Industry in the broadest sense of the term (for example collecting meteorological, banking and insurance data, and medicine, including increasingly complex medical devices, etc.) will just be a marginally free matter of processing information, involving humans only at the two ends of the chain: engineers at the beginning and unskilled workers at the end for the few tasks that robots cannot perform themselves. Those predicting the end of human labour even say that most forms of care, including those that theoretically require the most humanity, such as tending to the sick and aged, will soon vanish as well because of algorithms. It has already been seen that vulnerable people can develop real emotional bonds as easily with "nice" robots as with dogs, and certainly even more easily than with unpleasant human beings. Politics is also changing. Swift changes in these areas will meet with considerable social resistance, perhaps even sparking unrest, but the trend towards zero cost in information production will meet with equally fierce resistance to the abolition of income (from patents, for example), lack of transparency (individuals and groups have always wanted to protect themselves from prying eyes; that is part of human nature) and the Orwellian prospect of a life run by a supreme computer setting costs and distributing revenue. People will not accept having to live their lives in the glare of an inescapable spotlight.

If that is indeed what the future holds in store, the transition will be difficult, if not tragic. To make it as smooth as possible, we need to get organised, not just locally but also globally: that is a key aspect of global governance. The trend towards the concentration of information collection and processing infrastructure into one American "hand", or into two at the most, the other being Chinese, is not the least of the difficulties.

Between reality and fiction

We are told that in the world to come, men and objects will be bristling with sensors which, thanks to increasingly advanced real-time analytical processing of massive big data flows, will "optimize" every aspect of their existence, albeit based on external criteria that mankind will find increasingly hard to avoid. Here again, the spectre of Big Brother is looming.

Energy, information and logistics will be integrated into huge platforms. Buildings and cities will be "smart". Technologists are developing a veritable ideology that all of us will end up adopting. Men will increasingly produce their artefacts with 3D printers. These printers — if the word can still be used — will also be capable of remotely producing increasingly complex systems, including drones, cars (electric, driverless, flying and multi-connected), and why not aircrafts and rockets one day.

Robots that will increasingly look and act like humans will assist machines and men in every facet of their daily lives.

Let's make a pass on bugs, viruses and other endogenous or exogenous (hackers, etc.) problems, although such questions are already being asked and digital disasters are expected to occur sooner or later. By merrily clearing hurdles, a dream of "progress" is emerging at such a dizzying pace that it will be hard to tell androids apart from humans. Real people, after undeniable challenging transition periods, will be completely freed from industrial tasks, i.e. those based on reproduction or imitation. But they will still possess their latitude of creation, which Bergson saw as the essence of the vital impetus and of duration; as well as perhaps of wisdom, perhaps not. In fact, they will not have a monopoly on creativity, for machines will also acquire that ability, at least in certain areas. Having solved the economic problem of scarcity once and for all, men will be able to focus their vital impetus on the arts and the quest for beauty, goodness, truth and transcendence. This idea is not new, having already been found in Keynes.

Education, it is said, will be similar to MOOCs (Massive Open Online Courses), which are already common worldwide. As in the case of energy and information, the marginal cost of education will tend towards zero, but here again, confusion must be avoided. Until the day the announcement is made that science can be directly infused into brains, we poor humans will still have to make an effort to learn foreign languages or quantum mechanics. Most of us will still feel the need to interact with human professors. More generally, we must take the idea of knowledge as a public good with a grain of salt. Teaching is one thing, behaviour quite another. I cannot imagine either being cost-free — in other words without effort.

Technology romanticists and ideologues paint a bright future where all of those wonders will solve environmental problems. Anthropogenic global warming will be nothing but a bad memory. The course of the Anthropocene Era will have been deviated. The 20th century's medical strides give but a pale idea of what to expect, from brain-controlled prostheses (which already exist), to routine manufacturing of artificial organs (which is in the near future), remote non-intrusive surgery (which is almost here), unlimited repair of failing body parts, and the increase of cognitive capacity, etc. "Transhumanisation" is on its way.

Some go even further and claim that men will become immortal. Not really, however. Even somebody who has undergone countless repairs will no longer be mendable after a plane crash, a spacecraft explosion or a fight with other men — or robots! If men, or the robots that will partially replace them, remain mortal despite everything, it is because statistically, in the course of their theoretically eternal lives, an accident or war will inevitably claim them, even if at an advanced age (several million years, for example). Incidentally, perhaps suicide will become the normal end to an existence that will have become unbearable.

Looking beyond science fiction

Centuries from now, mankind will have reached a state of heightened consciousness thanks to the interconnection of brains and will die only from accidents, annihilation from other creatures or suicide. They will travel between galaxies in comfortable spacecrafts. Endless amounts of energy and information will let them travel at the speed of light and, consequently colonise exoplanets, perhaps after laying the groundwork first. Man will have learned how to remotely change distant worlds and transplant genetic programmes using electromagnetic waves or other means. The human race will spread across the universe, where it will certainly meet others, for why would life not have taken a similar course elsewhere? People will travel at the speed of general relativity. Einstein's theory will have become as palpable as Newton's laws are now. If, in the course of those colossal changes, the distinction between Good and Evil has not been abolished, transhumanisation can be imagined as though right out of a Star Wars movie for these human beings who will no longer be human.

The aim of the lines above is not to survey the feasible or far-fetched, bright or gloomy forecasts in books or magazines that capture the imaginations of technological romanticists, economic ideologues, dream merchants, artists of every stripe and hard-core atheists. A few of them are already coming true. More will follow, others will not. And things must be put into perspective. The conditions for a successful manned mission to Mars, as close as it is, remain distant. Many challenges must be overcome first, although they are not all clearly identified yet.

Let us at least show some humility and recognise that technology is not the answer to everything. Let us acknowledge how hard it is to make long-range forecasts in a system as complex as the tandem formed by mankind and Earth. Let us keep in mind that every deterministic theory of history, such as Marxism-Leninism, which was also an attempt to create a godless religion, has failed. Instead of speculating about a field that is too broad for guesswork, at this point I would rather return to the example of robots. There is no doubt that they will increasingly transform life in the upcoming years and decades, although their full impact remains only partly foreseeable.

The difficult question is that of "singularity", a word that qualifies a state where machines will have become "smarter" than men in every area. In 1995, American Ray Kurzweil published a book called *The Singularity is Near*. Machines already win at chess and even Go, which is a much subtler game, but those are very particular forms of intelligence[1], like that of the Hungarian mathematician Paul Erdős, who was famous for his extraordinary aptitude at mental calculation but seemed rather handicapped in everyday life.[2] To what extent can we speak of "intelligence" and not *types* of intelligence? Bergson made the case that man's creative capacity, minus that of calculation so to speak, is what sets him apart from other beings, which leads us to reformulate the idea of singularity. If he is right, will machines become more creative than people? This question seems inevitably vague. Creation inherently implies a leap into the radical unknown and it is impossible to paint an accurate picture of the future. How could such a vague question have a precise answer?[3]

Pursuing such a train of thought brings us to the age-old question of the nature of Consciousness, in its most fundamental sense. Consciousness with a capital "C" is sometimes referred to as "reflexive consciousness", as if such an expression could enlighten us. Consciousness is different from states of awareness, which can be more or less objectively defined. Anyone can speak of Consciousness in the same way that Saint Augustine spoke of

---

[1] This is a matter of combinatory intelligence, where the main problem lies in the number of combinations, but the nature of those combinations is theoretically predictable.

[2] Paul Hoffman, *The Man Who Loved Only Numbers*, Fouth Estate, London, 1998.

[3] Thus, in information theory, the possible acceptable answers to a given question must be totally identified in advance. For example, if a dice is cast, there are six possible answers, if we ignore the possibility that the dice might come to a rest balancing on an edge (12 cases) or a corner (8 cases).

Time with a capital "T" — that which is an inner experience and not the external time of clocks, daily life or, more sophisticatedly, of physicists, whose formulation can only be in a spiral and rely on mathematics. Saint Augustine said: *if I am not asked what it is, I know it; if I am asked, I do not know it*. Confusion regarding the subject of Consciousness among acclaimed futorologists, such as typically Kurzweil, is obvious. Jacques Monod completely exhausted the issue of Consciousness in his famous 1970 bestseller *Chance and Necessity*. Well before the emergence of androids and, even more so, contemporary robots, men questioned whether their peers were as aware as them, or whether they were merely machines, like the marble statue in Condillac's 1754 *Traité des sensations*. In 1950, Alan Turing put forward a test in which a human questioner converses simultaneously with another human and a computer, both out of view. According to Turing, if after a while the questioner can no longer tell them apart, it is because the machine is as "smart" as the man. In fact, his test reduces intelligence to language or, more specifically, to a limited set of language features. We are here very far from actual Consciousness.

When speaking with the most advanced robot, how can we tell whether or not it has a Consciousness? Neither the question, nor the answer is groundbreaking. The latter would most probably amount to observing the machine's reactions to certain questions asked with the intention of surprising it or its reactions to some of our attitudes: is the response absurd (in everyday language, someone is said to be "out of it") or out of sync? When two humans speak together, they exchange not just words, but also all sorts of non-verbal signs with endless nuances, starting with the gaze. And even words go beyond themselves. Any beginner in mathematical logic is asked to understand the need for a metalanguage, in this case a natural language[4] — hence the difficulty of a universal language, which captured Leibniz's attention. That also brings to mind the Frankenstein story, published in 1817, and the legend of the Golem (Hebrew for "shapeless matter"), which inspired films and books a century ago. In Paul Wegener and Karl Boese's eponymous 1920 German movie, the Golem, created for peaceful purposes, turns into a bloodthirsty demon, but a little girl's smile melts his heart.

In the end, we cannot avoid one radical question: how can one Consciousness recognise another and, consequently, beyond "intelligence", tell the difference between a human and the most advanced robot? More precisely, is it possible to design an algorithm that allows a machine to learn enough to *permanently* "fool" all of its human interlocutors, or even just one in every circumstance of its life? I doubt it, for algorithms are human achievements and men are more than their works. In more correct terms, perhaps, every human being lives inside his Consciousness, which is impervious to any external formulation, as is communication between Consciousnesses. But robots only

---

[4] At the start of his authoritative work *Mathematical Logic* (1967), Stephen C. Kleene advises those who cannot understand this point to give up on the idea of studying logic.

function with what is definable and universal signs.[5] That is true even for deep learning. And I have not yet addressed the issue of suffering, which is inseparable from that of Consciousness. Can a robot that suffers "physically", and above all "emotionally", and not just in appearance, still be called a robot? The following question — which is separate from Cartesian duality — must also be asked, because the matter of Consciousness seems to be connected with the idea of soul: how can a robot be animated? Etymologically, the verb "to animate" stems from the Latin *animare*, itself derived from *anima*: vital breath, soul. Is the soul, and with it the moral sense, an emerging property of energy-matter? Is it a necessary consequence of equations that have already been formulated or remain to be discovered, or does a principle exist that lies radically outside energy-matter but is likely to join forces with it in order to allow a spirit to spring forth? If souls live inside human bodies, can they decide to live inside robots?

My intention is not, of course, to claim to have an answer. Christianity speaks of the dual material and divine nature of humanity, Buddhism of reincarnation. They are two different, but not necessarily contradictory, ways of viewing Time. My goal is merely to show the need for transcendental reflection when technological speculation is taken a bit further. Is it not remarkable that we logically tend to invoke the body-soul-spirit

---

5   See H. Bergson, *Histoire de l'idée du temps,* Cours du Collège de France 1902-1903, PUF, 2016.

trilogy, which comes from the depths of time?[6] The matter is not so easy to dismiss. Can biology totally answer the question of life? Artificial intelligence raises all of those ancient questions anew, especially with regard to medicine, because bionic medicine has become a reality and is gradually extending to every part of the human body, including the brain. What can be said of the Ego of an animated robot or a bionic transhuman? How can ethics address the issue of transhumanisation?

---

6   This is one of the themes nurturing François Cheng's works.

Back to Earth

As humanity continues to embrace technology, it will face more immediate challenges than those posed by drone and robot warfare, or by the question of knowing whether machines will be tainted by original sin. If, like Fernand Braudel, we assign the word "civilisation" to the material realm and the word "culture" to our ways of living and thinking, then digital technology has obviously ushered in a new civilisation that tends to break with the past and has already spawned many myths and fantasies. The previous pages have attempted to sketch an outline of that civilisation. Will it *evenly* and, above all, *quickly* spread across the whole planet? Nothing could be less clear. Its progress, in both breadth and depth, comes up against economic, social and cultural hurdles that are likely to change its course here and there. The digital civilisation redistributes power,[1] typically to a handful of companies that collect and control data, relegating the industrial societies of the past to the rank of subcontractors. Google, Apple, Facebook, Amazon (GAFA) and Microsoft already have close ties with each other and with the United States government. They defy states. Meanwhile, states are also weakened by migratory movements, multiplied by the uncontrolled flows of information. The poor in impoverished countries and the victims in war-torn countries believe or hope that they will find salvation in wealthy countries without having to relinquish their cultural identity. As a result, the control of states over their own territory is dwindling. Some resist, trying to push back trends they deem undesirable by building real or virtual walls. Others see the gap between altruistic, politically correct discourse and reality growing wider every day, threatening to result in violence. Artificial intelligence is widening inequality, changing the nature of work and unleashing tidal waves of structural unemployment more seriously than any previous technological revolution did. The adaptation or protection systems set up in developed countries in the second half of the 20th century no longer fit the new reality, and the changes underway clash with all types of conservatism, if only due to their speed. Resistance may turn ugly. The emergence of new models such as the "collaborative economy", which typically

---

[1] On this subject, see "Qu'est-ce qu'une puissance au XXIe siècle" in Thierry de Montbrial, *La pensée et l'action, op. cit.*, pp. 635-660. This text is also on the website of the Académie des Sciences morales et politiques.

rocks the established foundations of taxation, is revolutionising how the economy works.

Digital civilisation will usher in a series of deep changes that are not always predictable or positive. The *system* — *Big Brother* — is getting savvier about all our resources and behaviours than we actually are. Everything we do, say or write is now stored without our knowledge and can be used against us at any time. As human nature has both a dark and light side, we all run the risk, sooner or later, of indictment, especially given the ease of taking information out of context. Moreover, broadly speaking, the safety and security of digital networks, whether they are linked to form or to content, are currently, and even more so potentially, problematic. The rise of social media has exacerbated the spread of rumours and conspiracy theories giving way to hostilities and violence. In national and international politics, emotions are prevailing over reason. The traditional ways and means of practicing liberal democracy are increasingly falling short. The legitimacy of leaders, stripped of their aura, is increasingly contested; their every move dissected under a microscope. Domestic and international law and, more generally, public institutions seem to be growing out of touch with current conditions with each passing day. Some peoples consider their culture to be under threat in the midst of this turmoil and are complaining about what they already perceive as ethnocides.

Writing these lines, I am not trying to identify all the problems of the great digital transition, much less to systematically dramatise the future, any more than I am claiming to list all the possible benefits that the future world has in store for us. I am merely trying to put across the idea that history marches on. In every period of time, the fears and expectations of a future already underway, and the memory and remnants of the past clash with each other like tectonic plates. The result can be violent. The coexistence of the wonders of technology, especially in Asia (considered underdeveloped until only recently), and of the resurgence of the most extreme forms of barbarism in countries that naïvely believed themselves to be definitively immune from war attests of the complexity of this world: at once home to "smart" cities on one side, the Islamic State on the other. How can we organise globalisation and harmoniously make the most of the digital civilisation's expected benefits if the legacy of the past is ignored? The next two chapters will address various aspects of this question.

Meanwhile, I have two reasons to end this chapter with the issue of religion. The first is to remind Man of his finiteness and to yield to humility. His ability to know is both immense and limited. Kant, the Enlightenment philosopher, did not believe that reason alone could provide access to knowledge, even of the scientific kind, as it is called today. This revelation led him to the idea of *categories of understanding*, which is still relevant — not in its modalities but in its principle. A fortiori, reason alone cannot answer metaphysical questions. In this sense, today's materialist rationalists are wrong when they claim the

Enlightenment philosophers as their spiritual forerunners. Kant postulated the universality of moral law, but he was Christian. Part of his genius lies in developing a system that theoretically allows everyone to obey moral law while leaving them free to believe in any religion or none at all. Like Bergson after him, the wise man of Königsberg bowed before Mystery. This is not the case with materialist rationalists such as 20th century Marxist-Leninists or the metaphysicists of AI and transhumanisation, who dream of manufacturing supermen and building power systems based on that utopia.

My second reason for discussing religion here is that, for many intellectuals, the mind-boggling progress of science and technology in the last two centuries had relegated them to the category of archaic belief systems. And yet, nobody can fathom the international situation in the early 21st century and beyond without understanding that religion also belongs to the future. Religion expresses the future as well as the past, which at first glance appears to be an enormous paradox.

The following remarks sum up four complementary points of view that I will call anthropological, ethnological, sociological and political. From the *anthropological point of view*, the immemorial experience suggests that most men, at least in certain circumstances of their lives, and to various extents, discern the existence of an impalpable reality beyond their senses. They express that in many ways, including the way they lead their lives and, often through art, as well as in the area of language, poetry: *I've seen, sometimes, what men only dreamed they saw* (Rimbaud). The holy books, such as the Bible or the Koran, are also poems.[2] With poetry, we are able to communicate the ineffable, thus building bridges with realities higher than those to which artificial intelligence could ever give us access. For many, religious feelings can be extremely vague and rare. Others are more or less credible witnesses to a more substantial access to higher realities. Sometimes, they found sects. Often, the witnesses are just relays who spread or keep up a faith. When a sect lastingly builds up a large enough number of credible members, it turns into a religion. The details of how religions start and grow matter little here. According to the *Book of Genesis*, God spoke to his people before Abraham. Christians believe Jesus is the Son of God, but his incarnation is part of a narrative, and therefore of human time. The founders of Buddhism and Islam were clearly human. Hinduism or Taoism, on the other hand, do not have identified founders. Despite what is often said, they are indeed religions, especially the latter. Like the Chinese word Qi, the word Tao (or Dao) is related to the Breath or Word of the three monotheistic religions. According to Saint John, at the root, God and the Word were/are one. *In the beginning was the Word*: this is the same as Logos, Breath, Qi. The "beginning" is not "zero hour", the "moment" of the Big Bang. It is the principle (in Latin: *in principio erat verbum*). The principle lies outside of Time. The Holy Spirit is at the heart of the Christian mystery of the Trinity.

---

[2] With regards to the Bible, see M. Edwards, *Bible et poésie*, Éditions de Fallois, 2016.

No religion can survive without a continuous influx of credible witnesses. True, some religions fade away, but their remnants can often be found in others. In Egypt, traces of the Pharaohs' religion can still be detected in Coptic Christianity and certain folk beliefs. In fact, there is a genealogy of religions. The main point is the relationship to transcendence. If men were cut off from that relationship, religions would vanish forever. The 20th century ideologies that claimed to sweep them away have failed. Will artificial intelligence succeed where they did not? I doubt it, for reasons I will explain in the next chapter.

In practice, a religion is manifested to varying degrees by an organisation, a doctrine and rites, accompanied by a moral code, or at least a body of wisdom. The opposite is not true. In other words, in the name of reason alone, it is possible, at least axiomatically, to separate morality from religion. As for the art of wisdom, it does not involve a relationship to transcendence as such.

Religions reflect transcendence filtered by man. They are therefore part of history. However, the history of humankind is not first and foremost that of individuals but of peoples, and it should come as no surprise if they have sought to create their own religious institutions, even if it results in futile distinctions on the most fundamental level. That brings us to the *ethnological point of view*, where religions are manifested as both fundamental attributes of identity and power systems, inevitably competing with state power. Ultimately, belief in, and worship of, a deity do not necessarily concord, except presumably intermittently. That is why world history is strewn with wars of religion, which are clearly still happening now. After the fall of the Soviet Union, the ethnic dimension of religion came back to the forefront. Orthodoxy has replaced communism in representing Russian national identity. Yet, this dimension had never truly disappeared for anyone who cared to look. In the Middle East, every political ideology imported from the West in the century after the fall of the Ottoman Empire has failed. In various forms, Islam has become a fundamental marker of quests for identity.

Then there is the *sociological point of view*. Religion, an attribute of identity, pervades the habits and, more generally, the cultures of peoples and nations: the calendar of rites and festivals, the landscapes (churches, mosques, pagodas, temples, cemeteries, etc.), the food, the clothing and especially literature and art. With multicultural states gradually replacing strictly ethnic realities (like the tribes of Africa, the Middle East or Asia) in the most economically advanced countries, cultural rivalry is on the rise in nations historically unprepared to welcome "diversity". In Western Europe, the Commonwealth's legacy made Great Britain an exception, although increasingly less so with the rise of terrorism. But a country such as France, still living on the myth of the "Republic one and indivisible", with a conception of secularism directly inherited from the quarrel between the Catholic Church and the Republican State around 1900, is helpless before a very different contemporary reality: communitarianism, which it allowed to grow and dares not look in the eye.

That leads us to the *political point of view*. If a nation's primary goal is to maintain the "will to live together", ethnic or cultural rivalries must be contained within narrow limits. Religions frown upon the advent of digital civilisation, or at least its unbridled materialism. Revolutionary new players, drawing mainly on Islam, which they manipulate, use all the resources of technology in order to achieve their aims. Lenin used to say capitalists would sell him the rope he would use to hang them. Likewise, the strategies of political Islamism are exploiting the weak links of multicultural societies, among which Western ones, to destabilise them, trigger chain reactions and impose their rule wherever they can. In that sense, the world is enmeshed in a conflict of civilisations and cultures that is more concrete for the future generations than a hypothetical Star Wars scenario several centuries from now or the prospect of an imminent apocalypse and the end of time, which was already at the heart of the earliest Christians' preoccupations. If we want the Anthropocene Era to be a happy one, this challenge must first be overcome. It is the major issue facing the early 21st century.

II
FOOTPRINTS FROM THE PAST

The usefulness of history

A quarter-century after the fall of the Soviet Union, the contrast of outlooks could not be more striking. On one hand, the accelerating technological revolution is ushering in a civilisation even more different than the industrial society of the previous centuries was from the agricultural era.[1] Change is so swift that we are fantasising about the dawn of a radically new world where the human Prometheus, having conquered time, space and matter, becomes master of his fate — or rather, of the apocalypse. On the other hand, more prosaically, the opposing Western ideologies that emerged after the Second World War — one advocating the welfare state, the other the minimal state — have run their course. Nothing remains of the Socialist International's utopian

---

1 On the concept of civilisation, see ch. 1 "Back on Earth" and Thierry de Montbrial, *La Pensée et l'action, op.cit.*, pp. 488 and following.

dream spawned by the 19th century's social transformations, safe for maybe the nostalgia for an anthem of an elder generation. The utopia of liberal globalisation that followed the dream of total socialism faded even faster. Both forms of utopia clearly have Christian roots. After the failure of "religions" without transcendence, while waiting for the failure of the "religion" of technology, the wretched of the Earth have no place left to turn but to ideologies explicitly based on religion. That has not been lost on the leaders they spawn. Participants at any major international CEOs conference celebrate knowledge, science and *Homo sapiens 2.0* while lambasting "false solutions like religions". They praise the virtues of leadership without questioning the reasons for the emergence of so many leaders who have been able to base their power on the masses by manipulating a religion — as it so happens that only they and very few of their followers have in fact internalised. A quarter-century after the great transition of the latter half of the 20th century, at a time when science and technology have never been so triumphant, religion is at the geopolitical forefront. And, instead of moving towards coordination, if not integration — as would entail the growing interdependence — national identities, and even more so, the international system are crumbling. A hundred years after the First World War, the start of the 20th century on a political level, everybody is wondering whether the 21st century will be much less radiant than the apostles of technology would have us believe.

All happy families are alike; each unhappy family is unhappy in its own way, Tolstoy wrote at the beginning of *Anna Karenina.* The same goes for peoples. In good times, they feel no need, except out of curiosity, to wonder about their "identity": it is self-evident. During darker days, they wonder who they are, what they must prevent, what must be saved and perhaps even what they would be willing to lay down their lives for. The quest for identity can strengthen but also divide them, as can be seen today in France or other European countries where the divergences between identity narratives are spreading. Paul Valéry was right to write in *Reflections on the World Today,* published in difficult times before the Second World War: *History is the most dangerous product evolved from the chemistry of the intellect. Its properties are well known. It causes dreams, it intoxicates peoples, gives them false memories, quickens their reflexes, keeps their old wounds open, torments them in their repose, leads them into delusions either of grandeur or persecution, and makes nations bitter, arrogant, insufferable and vain.* How a founding narrative of identity can become a ticking time bomb can still be seen nowadays. But in *Historical Fact,* Valéry also wrote that this discipline, *associated with the independence of the mind, [...] can help us to see.* He added that meditating on the past shows us *the frequent failure of predictions that are too precise, and, on the other hand, the great advantages of a general and constant preparation, which — without claiming to determine or defy events, for these are invariably surprising or develop surprising consequences — makes it possible for men to manoeuvre readily against the unexpected.* Valéry gives us arguments to nuance another of his maxims, just as famous, and on which I had to dissertate in high school: *History justifies whatever we want it to. It teaches absolutely nothing, for it contains everything and gives examples of everything.*

Yet history's usefulness as a science of action is obvious for politicians, diplomats or soldiers. Poor knowledge of *others'* history and geography is a major source of both domestic and foreign policy blunders, including chaotic immigration and military interventions that go awry. History, which today must be critically based on all the social and human sciences, is the ultimate science of government. But governments are less and less eager to cultivate history, as though law or economics, for example, could advantageously replace it. More generally, history is useful for all kinds of entrepreneurs because it can help them better understand their partners or competitors' behaviour — in other words their actions and reactions. Every management specialist in the broad sense of the term stresses the importance of "feedback", especially *a posteriori* error analysis. *History is the science of things that do not repeat themselves,* Valéry said. That is why calculating probabilities, at least in its most common form,[2] is useless to great leaders. But many lessons can often be drawn from comparing properly considered "things". Like so many other disciplines, history is not a homogeneous science. It is open to an *a priori* limitless number of approaches depending on the historian and his readers' interests. As an exercise of memory,

---

[2] The logic of reasoning in uncertainty surpasses the framework of repetitive situations. In the 20th century, a whole school of logic grew up around the idea of subjective probability, to which economic theorists have made some of the most important contributions.

it selects, distorts and reconstructs, but as a science, it relies on objective traces of the past and consequently does not allow all narratives to be considered equal. There is no unified theory of history any more than there is one overarching theory in physics or economics. Searching for one would be pointless. One aspect of history is to offer the man of action a wide range of case studies, giving him food for thought in order to increase his information in the precise sense given to that term in the previous chapters. The value of Clausewitz's great treatise, *Vom Kriege*, lies in the alliance between his skill at putting abstract ideas into words, his thorough knowledge of the Napoleonic Wars and his deep personal experience, making him one with his subject.

If President George W. Bush and his vice-president, Dick Cheney, had not succumbed to the ideology of the Greater Middle East, marked by an abysmal lack of knowledge about the region and its history, chaos would not have spread as widely as it did, setting off a chain reaction of disasters in the Middle East and, on another level, in Europe. In another example, if Western leaders had better understood the history of Russia and the trauma it experienced during the 1990s, they would have trodden more carefully in their intention to militantly extend Euro-Atlantic institutions to the borders of Georgia or Ukraine. A new version of the Cold War, certainly less intense but nevertheless debilitating for Europe, probably would have been avoided, allowing them to focus instead on the 21st century's key geopolitical issue: the rivalry between the United States and China against a backdrop of fierce competition for technological dominance. That rivalry should bring Europe's countries closer together if they aim to continue playing a role in history. In both cases, the West's mistake consisted of defining other peoples' interests in their place. Those examples also show how thorny the issue is. Two of history's above-mentioned facets interfere with each other: on the one hand, Valéry's chemical of the intellect, which, in this case, enflamed part of Western public opinion and spread the idea that by toppling regimes, whether Saddam Hussein's in Iraq or, possibly after the "liberation" of Ukraine, Putin's in Russia, a big step would have been taken towards a "happy" globalisation; on the other, the foolishness of governments, gripped by ideology or petty calculations, regardless of the facts. The "lessons of history" that in my opinion, can be legitimately drawn from this kind of episode include the certainty of great danger when governments stoke popular passions, while, on the contrary, their mission is to act, inasmuch as possible, in knowledge of the facts and under the empire of moderation.

That is the essence of realism, which, unjustly, is often confused with cynicism. Far from it, realism is not incompatible with referring to a moral compass, the only possible long-term guide in the fog of action.[3] Mistakes can be made in every case. Clausewitz stressed the importance of the fog of war, but that of politics is often no less thick. As the eminent Indian diplomat

---

3 Machiavelli wrote that moral principles must not dictate the way of governing, but nor should governments allow impulses and passions to influence their behaviour. See Thierry de Montbrial and Thomas Gomart (ed.), *Notre intérêt national*, Odile Jacob, 2017, p. 6.

Shivshankar Menon superbly showed,[4] governments' choices seldom resemble operational research theorists' "options". How they are presented to decision-makers largely depends on circumstances. But a poor grasp of history always, and sometimes critically, raises the risk of making mistakes. Convinced of that, two great observers of the international scene, English historian Niall Ferguson and American political scientist Graham Allison, proposed setting up a Council of Historians to advise the President of the United States, similar to the influential Council of Economic Advisors. That was before Trump's election on 8 November 2016. There is little chance of the administration's new team, laden with self-assurance, accepting the recommendation.

In the rest of this chapter, and in the following one, I propose surveying certain aspects of 20th and early 21st century history to draw some, in my opinion, relevant lessons with a view towards safeguarding, in the coming years and decades, the chances of a *reasonably open* and peaceful planet, despite the inevitable turbulence. In this speech, I want to suggest that the time has come to dispel the utopian idea of a flat, borderless world governed by the wisdom of multinationals concerned with the "global public welfare" and steeped in their "social responsibility" but completely unattached to any country. I also want to stress that a return to barriers between peoples, curtailment of exchanges of every nature and a widespread climate of mistrust would be so contrary to the

---

[4] S. Menon, *Choices: Inside the Making of Indian Foreign Policy*, Brookings Institution Press, Washington DC, 2016.

natural tendency of the technological revolutions underway that it could only lead to a great catastrophe whose modalities, details or, naturally, timing would be unpredictable.

History's numerous facets include the hindsight approach, which involves travelling back in time instead of bringing it to us, in search of past events that may shed light on the present and immediate future. This approach recalls psychoanalysis and must be taken with the same grain of salt. I will not dwell on the difficulty of the notion of event, which is usually based on the systemic reconstruction of a group of objectively identifiable basic facts. As in quantum physics, there is a sort of interaction between the observer and the phenomenon observed in history. Since history has no starting point, a time limit must be chosen in any retrospective approach, although such limit may be pushed farther back in time when necessary. In geopolitics, 1945 seems like a good year to date the start of the contemporary world because it marks the beginning of a period that lasted until 1989-1991, the end of which still influences today's world. But it is often indispensable to include the whole 20th century, for many of the contemporary world's characteristic features can only be understood by looking back at the First World War peace treaties and beyond.[5]

---

5 See Thierry de Montbrial, *Mémoire du temps présent*, Flammarion, 1996.

Scientific, technological and economic roots of the contemporary world

There is one area in which it appears necessary to explicitly go back to the early 20th century. This will also give us an opportunity to strengthen the links between the various chapters of this short essay. The area in question is the scientific and technological revolution, whose unprecedented speed and scale have relentlessly increased, changing how human beings perceive their place in the cosmos.

By the turn of the 19th century, physicists had, certainly, made amazing breakthroughs compared to Kant's time, to the point where most of them believed that an unsurpassable peak had been reached. But mental images of space, time, matter and energy were basically the same as they had been in Königsberg's categories of understanding. Or, to paraphrase Bergson, the whole Cosmos could be grasped by the immediate data of consciousness.

The theory of relativity and quantum mechanics in particular, as well as information theory (albeit in a different way), have not just led to a radical paradigm shift, but also suddenly capsized the consciousness of the intimate relationship between human beings and the visible and invisible universe. That fabulous revolution of the mind was over by the Second World War. None of the later developments in the natural sciences had as much impact, including culturally, with the exception of the discovery of the genetic code in the early 1950s.

The first revolution started with Albert Einstein and his theories of special (1905) and general (1916) relativity. In the relativist paradigm, the space-time continuum forms an inseparable four-dimensional geometric whole curved by matter-energy, which can turn into each other, as I recalled above. From the philosophical point of view, the most extraordinary thing about the theory of relativity is undoubtedly the disconnection that it implies between the reality of physicists' time and the time of human consciousness, which is reduced to an intersubjective agreement with a narrowly limited scope. In that regard, it is easy to see why the misunderstanding between Einstein and Bergson was total.[1] Einstein was only marginally interested in philosophy. Bergson, despite an honourable scientific education, was unable to think in the same way as the physicist who invented (or discovered?) relativity. The debate is not completely over yet,

---

[1] Historians have written about the debate between them at the Collège de France on 6 April 1922. It was a dialogue of the deaf. See Jimena Canale, *The Physicist and The Philosopher*, Princeton University Press, 2015.

insofar as it is not impossible that Bergson's concept of duration as the latitude of creation also has relevance in cosmology. In other words, the "universe" may also be a subject of history. In any case, special relativity has already changed the world with nuclear power and revolutionised astrophysics, notably by allowing us to understand nuclear fusion inside stars. General relativity is the theoretical basis of cosmology, an embryonic discipline prior to Einstein. Its latest prediction to be experimentally verified (in 2016) is the phenomenon of gravitational waves, a tremendous achievement not just of science, but also technology.

Relativity clearly has one founder, but quantum mechanics, at least in its heroic phase, was more of a collective work, featuring great names such as France's Louis de Broglie, Germany's Werner Heisenberg, Austria's Erwin Schrödinger and of course Einstein, with his theoretical explanation of the photoelectric effect.[2] In the quantum paradigm, in the absence of measurements, the values defining a particle's location in space-time (typically the coordinates and quantity of movement) only exist in probability, in a very precise mathematical sense. It is impossible to simultaneously measure two values such as those just mentioned with exactitude. Heisenberg expressed that fact in the famous "uncertainty principle" he formulated in 1927. In quantum mechanics, it is not the space-time framework but the interpretation of its contents (matter, light, *in fine* the elementary

---

[2] See, for example, Jim Bagott, *The Quantum Story: A History in 40 Moments*, Oxford University Press, 2011. It is often forgotten that Einstein was awarded the 1921 Nobel Prize in physics for his work on the photoelectric effect, not relativity.

particles) and their behaviour that defies what is usually called common sense. *I think I can safely say that nobody understands quantum mechanics,* wrote Richard Feynman, another giant of 20th century physics, who made major contributions to the field.[3] Thus, the quantum world is full of "paradoxes" that are still being debated. One of the most impressive is "delocalisation", proven experimentally, according to which a single particle can be in two different places in space at the same time. That phenomenon, which is hard for anybody with little inclination for abstract thought to fathom, could "explain" certain states of consciousness in human beings. Quantum mechanics is fascinating in that regard, but also because of its unifying power at the fundamental level. It revolutionised chemistry by completely explaining the structure of atoms (the image of an electron revolving around a nucleus is incompatible with classical mechanics) and molecules (chemical bonding, which was still mysterious until then). This was the starting point for the work of Linus Pauling, who won the Nobel Prize for chemistry in 1954 and peace in 1962 for his nuclear disarmament campaign. Quantum mechanics has also been successful in high-energy and particle physics. It is the basis of the "standard model", which unifies three of the four fundamental forces of nature (electromagnetic interaction, strong and weak nuclear interactions), but attempts to achieve

---

[3] *The Character of Physical Law* (MIT Press, 1965), p. 129. Feynman often wrote about this topic. For a philosophical overview of quantum mechanics, see Bernard d'Espagnat *Le réel voilé, analyse des concepts quantiques,* Fayard, 1994; *Traité de physique et de philosophie,* Fayard, 2002; and (with Claude Saliceti), *Candide et le physicien,* Fayard, 2008.

total unification — that is to say, to include gravity — have been unsuccessful, despite the ultra-sophisticated developments of string and "superstring" theory.[4]

The time has now come to discuss another revolution, which took place in the narrowest circle of mathematicians: that of logicians. By the turn of the 19th century, mathematics had also reached new impressive levels of accomplishment, often through the ongoing exchange with physicists and their new foundings. Incidentally, one of the most fascinating aspects of the history of science is the sort of dance that mathematicians and physicists ceaselessly perform, one group following, the other leading, depending on circumstances. Examples include relativity or quantum mechanics with Riemannian geometry or Hilbert spaces. But what I am going to focus on now is a completely different matter. Around 1900, some mathematicians, including David Hilbert, were intent in providing stronger axioms to their discipline, concerned their structures would collapse one day due to paradoxes and inconsistencies left unnoticed in the foundation of mathematics. Among the chief figures involved in that endeavour is English philosopher Bertrand Russell, who, with Alfred North Whitehead, wrote a book with a significant impact on philosophy, *Principia Mathematica* (1910). Russell was among the first to show apparently very simple logical paradoxes, such as the contradictions that result when speaking of "the set

---

4   For a relatively accessible work, see Paul Langacker, *Can the Laws of Physics be Unified?*, Princeton University Press, 2017.

of all sets".[5] That marked the emergence of a new scientific field: mathematical logic, a vast extension of the Aristotelian logic with which philosophers had been satisfied until then. Analytical philosophy, which is interested in all the forms of language, is anchored in this type of approach. The extensive study of this new discipline led to highly disturbing outcomes, such as Kurt Gödel's famous theorem, published in 1931. One of mathematical logic's first tasks was to provide a solid, and above all, non-contradictory base for the theory of natural whole numbers (1, 2, 3, etc.), such as Peano's axioms. Gödel had the idea, which may seem odd to the average man, to question whether such axioms could prove all truths about the arithmetic of natural numbers. Surprisingly, he established that the answer to this question is negative. In other words, in a framework as seemingly simple as that of natural numbers, there are true but improvable results! Although Gödel's theorems (there was not just one) did not stir public debates as passionate as those triggered by relativity or quantum mechanics, at the level of the philosophy of knowledge, it did shake existing certitudes to which mathematicians had become accustomed in the name of intuition.

For the interested reader, let us add a few words on one of the greatest enigmas in the history of mathematics: "Fermat's conjecture". Any middle school student knows the Pythagorean theorem: in a right triangle, the square of the hypotenuse (the

---

5   For example, by admitting the existence of the set of all sets, one immediately sees that the set of sets that do not belong to themselves can neither belong nor not belong to itself. If you feel disconcerted by this observation, do not worry and keep reading!

side opposite the right angle) is equal to the sum of the squares of the other two sides. If, for example, those two sides are 3 and 4 cm long, respectively, the length of the hypotenuse is 5 cm (3 squared is 9; 4 squared is 16; 9 + 16 = 25 = 5 squared). Generally, by naming the hypotenuse z, and the other sides x and y, the Pythagorean theorem is written $x^2 + y^2 = z^2$. If x = 1 and y = 1, then $z^2 = 2$. But it is quite easy to demonstrate that no change of unit exists (from centimetre to millimetre or micron and so forth) that can in this case make the hypotenuse measurable by an integer. It is said that the square root of 2 is irrational. This situation is the rule rather than the exception. At this point, it is worth underscoring that terminology is important in the sciences. The square root of 2 is irrational because, in view of the above, it does not identify with a ratio of two integers, and numbers in such a ratio are called rational. However, the word irrational also suggests "contrary to reason". Mathematicians have also been led to introduce entities such as negative numbers possessing a square root, calling them "imaginary numbers". But these new numbers are no more nor less imaginary than the others, so today the term "complex numbers" is preferred. The important point is that, in the sciences, wrong terminological choices can be misleading. One immediately thinks of the word "intelligence" in Artificial Intelligence, or the quasi-mystical vocabulary of molecular biology. A beautiful study could be made of this subject. But let us return to Pythagoras and what came after him. It is natural to wonder about the existence of solutions in integers of the equation $x^3 + y^3 = z^3$ and, more generally, $x^n + y^n = z^n$ [(x to the power of n) + (y to the power of n) = (z to the power of n)] for the sequence of natural numbers n = 3, 4, 5, etc. In the 1630s, French mathematician Pierre de Fermat claimed, in the margins of a copy of Diophantus' *Arithmetica*,[6] that he had demonstrated that these equations have no solution in integers although he did not provide any "proof". The greatest mathematicians tried to solve the problem. As surprising as it may seem, they only obtained partial results, but along the way developed new methods of great interest to science trying to demonstrate Fermat's conjecture, for which no counter-example had ever been found. It was not until 1995, 358 years after Fermat first posed the problem, that English mathematician Andrew Wiles announced a solution at the end of an incredible saga.[7] That solution drew upon a huge mathematical arsenal, well beyond arithmetic, that obviously had not been available to his illustrious predecessor. There are still many other unproven conjectures in number theory. Some may remain improvable within the framework of arithmetic but find a solution within a wider one. As we shall see, the question has concrete aspects.

The plot thickens when the most basic aspects of artificial intelligence, discussed in the previous section, enter the picture. It becomes natural to draw an analogy between the logician's

---

6 This book was written between 150 BCE and 350 CE.
7 See Simon Singh, *Fermat's Last Theorem: The Story of a Riddle that Confounded the World's Greatest Minds for 358 Years*, Fourth Estate, London, 1997.

approach, which starts out with calculations based on "proposals" taken as wholes that can only be true or false, and that of ordinary calculation, which operates with numbers. While Gödel was producing his results, Alan Turing was designing a virtual machine theoretically capable of performing every conceivable calculation, or, more precisely, executing every imaginable algorithm. Turing was not concerned with efficiency — whether the calculation took one minute or centuries mattered little to him — but feasibility. But an algorithm can run indefinitely without ever producing any results. It is easy to see that the machine version of Gödel's theorem is the existence of exact results but towards which no algorithm can converge whatever the length of time (in other words, in a finite number of steps). Incidentally, Turing is one of those figures the general public is interested in less for their contribution to thought than for the eccentricity of their lives. People from as widely varying backgrounds as Evariste Galois, Bertrand Russell, Albert Einstein and John Maynard Keynes also fall into this category.

I have already referred to the rich and complex reciprocal relationship between physics and mathematics.[8] The same goes for the ties between basic science, which includes those disciplines, and technology. The history of mechanics, thermodynamics,

---

[8] At a famous conference during the international congress of mathematicians in Paris in 1900, David Hilbert, mentioned above several times in the present essay, listed 23 unsolved problems that he deemed fundamental. Problem 6 involves the axiomatic treatment of the laws of physics. It is worth noting that, although Fermat's conjecture was mentioned at the beginning of the conference, it was not included in the list of problems. For Hilbert, its interest was only indirect, and he was right. See Jeremy J. Gray, *The Hilbert Challenge*, Oxford University Press, 2000.

optics and electricity — the four main branches of physics at the turn of the 19th century — provides many examples. In particular, I am thinking of the relationship between the study of the steam engine and the development of the second law of thermodynamics from Watt to Clausius.[9] It is fair to say that all the technology from the early 20th century until the Second World War, including, naturally, the automobile and aviation, was essentially based on the paradigms of physics in its most advanced state around 1900.[10] Under pressure from American strategists during the Second World War, the new physics began to emerge, first in the field of nuclear science (the atomic bomb, nuclear reactors), then in the development of "electronic calculators".

Those two adventures tapped some of the best minds of the time. I would like to mention one in particular, the Hungarian-born American John Von Neumann, a multidisciplinary genius who died prematurely in 1957. A prolific mathematician, author of important works on quantum mechanics and computer science trailblazer, he made key contributions to the design of the earliest electronic calculators (Von Neumann invented the "architecture" still used for most computers today[11]) and was an artificial intelligence pioneer with his work on automatons and conviction

---

9   See D. S. L. Cardwell, *From Watt to Clausius*, Heinemann, London, 1971.

10 See Trevor I. Williams, *A Short History of Twentieth Century Technology*, Oxford University Press, 1982. This book is about technology in the first half of the 20th century. With regard to the first rockets, Germany's Werner von Braun played a key role in launching NASA in the United States after the war. See Bob Ward, *Dr. Space. The Life of Werner von Braun*, Naval Institute Press, Annapolis, Maryland, 2005.

11 See V. Aspray, *John Von Neumann and the Origins of Modern Computing*, the MIT Press, 1990.

that computers and the human brain function in similar ways. His posthumously published book *The Computer and the Brain*, mainly of historical interest today,[12] addresses a key issue that continues to divide artificial intelligence specialists into two camps: exponents of "weak" artificial intelligence, for whom the computer is a means to simulate the brain's performance and test hypotheses involving its operating processes; and "strong" artificial intelligence, convinced that a computer can be programmed to make it equivalent to the human brain and all its mental activities.[13]

Artificial intelligence is obviously less and less "weak", but nothing suggests it will ever become "strong". "Strong" artificial intelligence is merely a philosophical posture, like Leibniz's fruitless search for an *ars characteristica* that, if it existed, would even make it possible to solve philosophical problems. If I mentioned Von Neumann, it is also because he founded, with economist Oskar Morgenstern, game theory, which aims to mathematically model situations of interdependence between a given number of adequately diagrammed players and analyse the possible forms of their interaction as well as the ensuing results depending on their resources, strategies, willingness to take risks, the information they have, etc. Game theory, which has advanced considerably since then, has become a basic tool for economists and strategists.[14]

---

12 J. Von Neumann, *The Computer and the Brain*, Yale University Press, 1958.
13 See M. Flasiński, *op. cit.*, pp. 235 and following. J. R. Seale introduced the terminology in 1980.
14 J. Von Neumann and O. Morgenstern, *Theory of Games and Economic Behavior*, Princeton University Press, 1944.

The exciting groundwork for what was later called artificial intelligence obviously affected biology. In his memoirs, *The Secret of Life*, James D. Watson, who co-discovered the double helix and the genetic code,[15] tells how *What is Life?*, a book by Schrödinger based on a 1943 series of lectures in Dublin (where he had found refuge) put him on the right track. In this short work, which had a considerable immediate impact, Schrödinger, a giant among the founding fathers of quantum mechanics, pondered the age-old question of whether the laws of physics can "explain" life.[16] Reproduction and self-organisation are two fundamental life processes. What captured Watson's imagination is that chromosomes appear to carry information through molecules that seem to form a sort of alphabet of coded messages. Writing and transmitting those messages would explain both processes. The code itself, its physical structure as well as that of messages, messengers and receivers, the structure made by every living thing — all that, Watson believed, was made with the same chemical building blocks, thus forming an integrated whole. At the time, DNA was already thought to play a key role, but it is the discovery of the double helix in 1953 that marked the start of molecular biology and the extraordinary adventure that followed. *What is Life?* raised another issue, which drew less notice at the time: life unfolds against the tendency to disorder — in other words, against the law of entropy. If, like Schrödinger, we call negentropy the

---

15 James D. Watson, DNA: *The Secret of Life*, Alfred A. Knopf, New York, 2003.
16 E. Schrödinger, *What is Life?*, Cambridge University Press, 1944.

opposite of entropy, it will be said that a living being's activity necessarily causes an increase in entropy in its environment that is greater than that of its own negentropy. All modern biology — that is, since the mid-20th century — is based on the validation of Schrödinger's hunches, with waves of consequences that are still very far from having run their course in medicine (including, naturally, pharmaceuticals), food and other industries where biological agents are likely to play a role. Major advances in brain science are also based on these paradigms.

Yet, can it be said that the "secret" of life, which apparently lies in the framework of the laws of physics as they are presently known, has definitively been found? There are at least three interdependent reasons to doubt this. The first is that the indefinable Consciousness remains radically unexplained. Roger Penrose, a giant of cosmology in the second half of the 20th century, relies on Gödel's theorems to refute the "strong" artificial intelligence thesis. He believes in the existence of still-unknown laws of physics that may shore up the foundations of biology.[17] The second is that the success of molecular biology lies in how efficiently it describes the molecular dynamics at work to form the basis of life and its observable or predictable effects, but does not explain it, and nobody knows yet how such factories were able to emerge from the primordial soup. True — and this is the third

---

17 See R. Penrose, "Why new physics is needed to understand the mind", ch. 9 by Michael Murphy and Luke O'Neill ed., *What is Life? The Next Fifty Years, Speculations on the Future of Biology*, Cambridge University Press, 1995. References to Penrose's earlier works dealing with the same question can also be found.

point — there is the theory of natural selection and evolution. But here again, that theory is more a perfectly calibrated language to describe and, to a much lesser extent, predict the evolution of species, while the above question is more valid on the scale of cosmological time: the entire chain of life since its "origins" seems radically improbable, unless an unknown metacode is assumed to exist. Another point can be added to those three: life itself is still imperfectly defined. Reflections of that kind have led some scientists to consider the necessity of developing a concept of information that would not be a sort of adjunct to logic, mathematics or physics, as it has been for nearly a century, but a fundamental physical reality necessary for a more relevant reformulation of the laws of nature.[18]

In the previous pages, I attempted to summarise some of the scientific, technological and cultural ideas that marked the 20th century and pervade the 21st. Their impact is increasingly felt in the economic and social order. I will conclude with some very brief remarks on that subject.

The *extensive growth* characterising phases of slow technological development gave way to the *intensive growth* characterising the United States and Europe after the war, with which the Communist countries, starting with the Soviet Union, proved incapable of keeping up, setting the stage for their own demise. By the 1960s, it was already impossible to doubt that the

---

[18] See Sara Imari Walker, Paul C. W. Davies and George F. R. Ellis, ed., *From Matter to Life*, Cambridge University Press, 2017.

question of "calculation" was posed well beyond the scope of digital analysis, the science of solving equations with figures, and stretched to the *a priori* unlimited area of "information processing", so that computer technology became the discipline of information or "digital" technology in the broadest sense of the term. As we have seen in the previous section, it also gradually became clear that, at the end of the day, the economy's most fundamental resources are energy and information, and that they are partially interchangeable. The digital revolution took place in several successive waves. The Internet, which started out as an interconnection between computers, continues to spread. Another revolution, blockchains, may be on the way. It would lead to the elimination of all the "trustworthy intermediaries" in transactions.[19] Those waves hastened the pace of globalisation — we will come back to that in the next chapter — but not to the point of making it completely irreversible. Human groups, peoples and nations are not dissolving in the ocean of technology. They do not mature at the same rate, and not just for the wrong reasons. And not all of them bear the brunt of the economic and social effects the same way.

---

19 See Don and Alex Tapscott, *Blockchain Revolution*, Portfolio/Penguin, 2016.

Modernity and progress

Looking back, it is clear how much humanity has been shaken since the early 20th century, first in the area of the mind, through the scientific and technological revolution discussed above, which is the basis of "modernity". American historian William Everdell had the brilliant idea of bringing together, in a single work, chapters on people as seemingly different as some of the mathematicians and physicists already mentioned in this essay; other scientists, such as Santiago Ramón y Cajal, who discovered neurons; painters, including Seurat, Kandinsky or Picasso; composers, like Schoenberg; and others.[1]

Alas, real modernity was manifested in the 20th century's two world wars. The first, sometimes still called the Great War, was not enough to make international politics realistic and

---

[1] William R. Everdell, *The First Moderns*, The University of Chicago Press, 1997.

reasonable. The Holocaust was also an example of real modernity, although nobody can claim to totally "explain" it: the viewpoints are so diverse that a convincing single theory is impossible to formulate. In the language of Cournot, it would be said that several more or less independent causal series intersected. The most recent publications that have drawn my attention on this subject include historian Johan Chapoutot's research on Nazi culture.[2] He demonstrated that Nazism was a structured *cultural revolution* to which thousands of journalists, writers, lawyers, legal experts, professors, scientists, ideologues, etc., actively contributed. Hundreds of thousands of people, often highly "cultivated", backed this cultural revolution, portrayed as the return to Germanic roots. Many behaved like Dr Pannwitz, Primo Levi's boss at Auschwitz. Levi, Chapoutot recalls, described his meeting with Pannwitz: *That look was not one between two men; and if I had known how completely to explain the nature of that look, which came as if across the glass window of an aquarium between two beings who live in different worlds, I would also have explained the essence of the great insanity of the third Germany. The fact is that Nazism was a body of ideas that were fairly convincing and relevant enough to many contemporaries to lead them to agree, join and act.*[3] What's more, *those ideas were chosen by individuals who were convinced that they were the right answers to the questions, problems and evils*

---

2 J. Chapoutot, *La révolution culturelle nazie*, Gallimard, 2017.
3 *Ibid.*, p. 17.

*of the time.*⁴ Chapoutot concludes his introduction as follows: *Why go into what Georges Mosse called "the eye of Nazism"? Quite simply, to do history. And to understand why and how men could see other men through the glass of an "aquarium."*⁵ Chapoutot writes useful history, for the horror of nazism recalls that no "progress" is irreversible, that in some circumstances a minority of fanatics can impose its will on a passive majority because they are satisfied, in this case with *the return to political and social order, trains that ran on time and better living standards, even a form of well-being, that the nazis' social policy brought about, not to mention the economic practice of the spoliation of non-indigenous people.*⁶ Like Raymond Aron in his *Memoirs,* how can one not continue to be surprised that a nation as civilised as Germany could have been as barbaric as today's jihadists? The "bad treaty" of Versailles and the Great Depression are often mentioned, rightly, to explain Hitler, but they do not tell the whole story. The spectre of the Holocaust will probably continue to haunt the world for a long time, if only by maintaining the Israeli exception in the international system. In my view, the most important thing to always keep in mind is that even the most advanced peoples are capable of barbarism. Human beings have both good and evil inside themselves. From a global perspective, the Holocaust was a European phenomenon, but since then the world has seen many other tragedies, including

---

4 *Ibid.*, p. 18.
5 *Ibid.*, p. 19.
6 *Ibid.*, p. 18.

the civil wars in Cambodia in the mid-1970s and in the Great Lakes 20 years later, which Westerners did nothing to stop even though they did not contribute to it. The first world war had already left behind a sense of absurdity, pervading the work of many writers and artists, which added to the loss of bearings caused by the growth of scientific knowledge. Can technologist ideology, which is very strong today, assuage the threat that the world associates, for the third time on a large scale, with the world wars and globalisation?

As Valéry would have said, any precise prediction in that regard would be futile. To answer indirectly, I will take up one of the most basic questions asked since the Age of Enlightenment: what is progress? The subject's difficulty stems from the fact that one often claims to establish a relation of order (one object of thought is either superior, inferior or equal to another) although neither the group of objects in question nor the comparison criteria has been clearly defined. It is therefore necessary to start by specifying the objects being considered. They cannot all be put into a single category.

The simplest case is mathematics, natural sciences and technology, considered from the perspective of knowledge alone. Take any discipline of this kind, like physics. It proceeds by successively increasing and reorganising a stock of knowledge. The validity of a proposition such as "physics progressed in the 20th century" is logically irrefutable.

But if the perspective is widened, for example by asking

whether the discovery of nuclear energy was a step ahead for humanity, the situation is trickier. Some people, including the author of this essay, believe that nuclear weapons allowed the Cold War to have a peaceful outcome. However, not only does such a proposition's wording need to be more precise, but it is based on a set of more or less well grounded reasons and assumptions, so that its validity cannot have an absolute character, unless it is given the form of an axiom. Yet what characterises an axiom is that it can be legitimately rejected. In the same vein, today some people would consider any form of nuclear proliferation as a step backwards. Others consider India and Pakistan's possession of nuclear weapons a geostrategic stabiliser. The example of nuclear facilities is easier because we have a more objective view of their advantages (availability, cleanliness, etc.) and drawbacks (waste storage, possible accidents, etc.). However, regardless of the measures taken to limit risks, comparing those overall advantages and drawbacks inevitably involves hypotheses based on subjective probabilities with which one can always play to reach a conclusion such as "nuclear facilities mark a step forward" or the opposite.

In practice, the nuclear power example also shows that, when faced with the complexity of certain judgements, public opinion is prompt to inflame and cast rationality aside, randomly influencing policymaking.

What can be said, then, of the digital civilisation? Scientific and technological knowledge have made undeniable progress. Their advantages, for example in medicine, are considerable, despite sometimes producing thorny ethical issues (surrogacy for example). But blanket judgements hardly lend themselves to the ideal of logical purity. And what to make of the excessive libertarian ideology with regard to the Internet, the fabrication of fake news and the "post-truth", the manipulation of emotions and the rise of violence fuelled by social media? It is true that, in many cases, the problem comes less from technology than from the attitude of society, which is resigned to the normalisation of disinformation, name-calling and invective. The attempt at relativism is being yielded to without considering the possible disastrous consequences it might entail. And what about the massive destruction of jobs and the humiliation of those the digital civilisation has left behind, which may lead to revolutionary situations in countries where only the strong survive? What about extremist groups that, using all the resources of technology, exploit situations of collective distress to their benefit? Of course, it can be hoped that a new baseline equilibrium will emerge in the long term — in other words, a few decades. But at what price? Those remarks do not mean to suggest that any kind of "precautionary principle" would make the transition easier. They say you can't stop progress. The same goes for the digital revolution. History has no genetic code, nor will it ever fulfil a rationally conceived human plan. At the least, we must become aware of the difficulty of the notion of progress in its many knotty aspects, and learn to settle for the pragmatic search for forms of organisation allowing us to avoid the many pitfalls and find wise paths forward. The search must encourage peoples to find their identities again while remaining sufficiently open and tolerant towards each other.

Now let us turn our attention to cases where the objects of study are political and social institutions. This ratchets up the degree of difficulty a notch. It is easy, for example, to utter platitudes such as "democracy is the worst form of government except for all the others". That kind of sentence reflects the loss of bearings after all those that transmitted traditions shattered in the early 20th century. But what is really being said, when the political system under discussion has not yet been situated in space and time, when its operating methods have not yet been spelled out and when the alternatives, with their advantages and drawbacks — in their context — and, above all, the conditions of establishing them, have not yet been considered? Philosophically reasoning, like Kant, about moral principles to which a universal value is axiomatically attributed (typically the Universal Declaration of human rights) is one thing, but it is quite another to act in a particular geographical and historical context, always shrouded in the fog of uncertainty. People who are experienced at thinking deeply and acting practically either do not reason the same way depending on which they are doing, or become the most dangerous ideologues. That takes us back to the lessons of history and the idea that, in action, good judgement does not boil down to abstract reasoning alone or, in logician-speak, propositional calculation.

Those observations have very concrete implications. Flirting with the idea of regime change in the Middle East, or even in Eastern Europe after the fall of the Soviet Union, some Western countries (the United States under George W. Bush and, to a lesser degree, France under Nicolas Sarkozy and François Hollande) have contributed to a chaotic situation where it is hard to see progress.

Institutions can be instruments of progress, at least temporarily. I am thinking typically of the origins of European construction, with the Commission system. But institutions, like peoples and nations, are enmeshed in a history. They have lives of their own. Even when their existence is functionally explained (central banks, for example), their contributions to clearly identifiable progress depends on their past, their memory, their leaders and their circumstances. A good Constitution does not always make a good government, and few ministers are good, especially in times when the wind of demagogy is blowing. Good institutions are like reeds in shifting soil. They keep the soil from being washed away as long as their vigour holds out. The same is true of global governance, where the goal is to pragmatically, gradually build up an international system capable of keeping the world reasonably open. But, as complex as such a system may be, its long-term success will ultimately depend on the support of the political units on which its functioning depends, on the commitment and quality of those responsible for implementing it and, finally, on the adherence of public opinion. However, the history of the 20th and early 21st century amply shows that public opinion depends on which way the wind is blowing, and that sometimes the power of passing ideologies sweeps aside in its wake,

Modernity and progress

leaving only ruins and desolation behind. It essentially boils down to the same, reoccurring, point.

Writing these lines in 2017, how can the sorrowful spectacle of so many liberal democracies, rocked by scandals and incapable of selecting leaders fit to govern, not be criticised? These political regimes are implicitly based on postulates that sometimes express ideologies wrongly confused with the philosophical principles of democracy or human rights, which, certainly, are also postulates, but of a different kind. In concrete democracies, the implicit postulates can be contradictory. For example, the abolition of the death penalty, which many consider absolute, irreversible progress, could suffer a setback one day, even in a country like France, merely by a referendum. In French political ideology (or British, which is even more surprising), the referendum is the height of popular sovereignty and, until further notice, the most important decisions are made by simple majority. Brexit was decided by a toss of the dice. I will return to that point in the next chapter. The poor functioning in practice of certain liberal democracies — and their difficulty in coordinating with each other and with the rest of the world in order to achieve goals in the common interest, such as keeping the world reasonably open — almost mechanically helps to shore up illiberal regimes, not just in Turkey, Russia, China and some European Union countries, but elsewhere as well. One day, the false progress of democracy in the West may be considered partially responsible for a drift towards authoritarianism or, worse, new forms of fascism or dictatorship in the East. Those prospects, which are by no means inevitable, have a *déjà vu* quality about them. Here again, the history of the 20th century provides some food for thought.

When one speaks of political and social institutions, one also thinks of mores. To address that issue, it is necessary to take the same long view as historians. That makes it easier to see, as Karl Marx did in the 19th century, that science and technology — not any science or technology in particular, but the overall progress of knowledge and the interaction between them — are the main driving forces not only behind social change, but also, undoubtedly, behind the movement of "ideas". They spelt the end of slavery and allowed the emancipation of women. In that sense, history can incontestably be spoken of as progress. But in the long term, the ways, means and timetable of change — unpredictable with regard to the details — bring countless active units working for or against change into play. It is these ways and means that make the march of ideas and events[7] a highly uncertain, volatile process. Not all societies mature at the same rate. When those deemed the most advanced seek to impose their standards and pace on others, they risk causing, certainly inadvertently, more or less temporary geopolitical, economic or social cataclysms.

Marx, or rather Marxism-Leninism, made the mistake of seeing a deterministic interpretation of history in those kinds of considerations by relying on Hegel's abstractions to postulate the dawn of a radiant socialism and the withering away of the

---

7 I borrow this wording from Antoine Augustin Cournot: cf. *Considérations sur la marche des idées et des évènements dans les temps modernes*, published 1872, volume IV of his *Œuvres complètes* published by the Vrin bookshop (1973).

State. In one of those twists of fate common in history, the ideas of Marx and the 19th century utopian socialists came to fruition where it was least expected, Tsarist Russia, shaken by the First World War, which produced, with Lenin and then Stalin, one of the most decisive factors in the 20th century's march of events.

The issue of progress in the realm of mores seems even more complex in areas where science and technology intervene less directly, but that does not make their indirect role any less obvious. Marx had already undertaken the huge task of deconstructing the closed systems that still governed thought at the turn of the 19th century. Science and war dispelled all certitudes and laid the groundwork for what is now called the human sciences. One of the most compelling was psychoanalysis, whose origins with Freud date to the late 19th century, but which largely expanded in the context of the scientific, ideological and political developments in the first third of the 20th century. Initially rooted in neurology and psychology, psychoanalysis, already with Freud himself, branched out into other fields, such as anthropology and its derivatives ethnology or literary criticism. The French have stood out in those areas with major figures such as Claude Lévi-Strauss or Michel Foucault, to mention just two. All the human sciences share the goal of revealing things hidden behind individual or collective mores and beliefs. Sexual behaviour is one of the subjects that gradually lost its taboo status in the late 20th century in the Western countries. With the liberation of speech, homosexuality became socially acceptable, leading to many institutional consequences.

The societies at the forefront of this trend still have a long way to go to resolve all their contradictions. For example, the idea of the right to have a child may conflict with the child's rights when the child wants to find its biological parents; medically-assisted procreation or surrogacy raise ethical issues. In addition to matters touching on family law, with all sorts of more or less predictable social consequences, peoples and societies do not all mature at the same pace. As avant-garde as a people might consider itself, in the name of what could it claim the right to impose its views on other peoples, even if it is collectively convinced that those other peoples will come around to its point of view? Shallow knowledge of this wise principle in international relations can be an objective cause of the aggravation of conflicts between nations.

Back to religion

In the private sphere, the notion of progress relates to the inner life of all human beings from childhood to death, and brings into play a form of knowledge quite different from science. Is it necessary to recall that for Muslims the great jihad is every human being's fight against the evil inside him? The goal of the present essay is not to dissertate on this topic, but it brings us back to the issue of religion, which, obviously, interferes with all the previous developments. From an ethnological perspective (as defined in a previous chapter), religions are at the heart of the post-Soviet international system. They are back in the spotlight after having been cast aside during the previous phase. The fall of communist ideology, a godless religion that shaped the Soviet Union's identity, left a vacuum that the Russian Orthodox Church immediately rushed in to fill, reconnecting with a reality that is deeply rooted in the country's history after an over 70-year parenthesis. More generally, the dual South-North (Catholic-Protestant) and West-East (Catholic and Protestant on one side, Orthodox on the other) dimension is indispensable to understanding Europe today. Even more impressive, of course, is the spread of political Islam, the last resource of identity in Muslim states that failed to define themselves in relation to European categories after independence. The Ba'ath Party proclaimed itself a socialist and secular regime in Syria (Assad father and son) and Iraq (Saddam Hussein). That is why it long benefitted from active sympathies, especially in France. The new ideological wave is powerful. To varying degrees, political Islam plays a role in the Middle East's three biggest and oldest states: Egypt, where the Muslim Brotherhood is more than ever on a war footing; Iran, where the Shah's regime, perceived by most of the population as a foreign body imposed by the West, was overthrown in the late 1970s; and, more recently, Turkey, where President Erdogan's project is to reconnect his country with its religious roots, if not restore the rank it held during the great Ottoman period, without breaking with modernity. Islamic tradition makes no distinction between the state and religion, and it is not impossible that Ataturk's system, which once seemed unique but promising, has run its course. To that must obviously be added, the importance throughout the Middle East of non-state political units with a revolutionary essence, such as Al Qaeda, Al Nusra, ISIS and others, which intend to redraw the map not just of the region, but of the world.

Back to religion

The religions "of the book" are conservative by nature. They are based on difficult texts that are rooted in space and time but have a universal character, and on a set of traditions, also complex and marked by situations and circumstances. In the space of their spiritual lives, believers are more or less dependent on professionals called, in the broad sense of the term, "clerics", attached to institutions that are also diverse but where, as I recalled in the first part of this book, the spiritual and temporal are linked, sometimes inextricably.

From the standpoint of the Western countries (I am using this rather simplistic terminology for the sake of brevity), which have dominated the world stage since modern times, Islam raises two obviously interdependent problems. The first is the nature of its main source, the Koran, presented as a book dictated by God to a man, the prophet Mohammed, in a particular language, Arabic. Reading and understanding this book is all the harder because its form, which experts extol for its beauty, is poetic. It is impossible to imagine a machine translating the Koran, even with the best software. Only a poet can translate a poet, which amounts to writing another poem. A translation always bears the mark of spatial-temporal coordinates and of the translator's own genius. But God did not turn out to be a universal translator. That is the first difficulty, which is smaller for Jews and Christians, whose sacred books were supposedly inspired but not dictated by God with, perhaps, a few exceptions (the Ten Commandments). Naturally, that does not keep them from having their fundamentalists, in other words, groups that, without necessarily aspiring to become directly involved in political action, seek to impose their views of the world, condemning fellow believers for whom time has moved on.

The second problem, which can be seen as an outgrowth of the first, is Islam's attitude towards scientific and technological progress, which is not specific to that religion. Christians recall the conflict between the Church and science, which was even more painful than the more recent rift between Church and state, neither of which has ever been totally resolved. Need we remind ourselves that in 1616 Pope Paul V condemned heliocentrism as contrary to Scripture and that, after Copernicus, the Inquisition condemned Galileo? The Church continued to make its voice heard. Darwin's ideas, published in 1859, met with fierce opposition. Powerful Christian groups still campaign against the theories of natural selection and evolution, dogmatically clinging to a literal interpretation of the *Book of Genesis*. Relativity, quantum mechanics and molecular biology have shaken conservatives even more than Copernicus' findings. The discovery of the double helix and biology's stunning progress starting in the mid-20th century were a blow to vitalism; a doctrine that claims that living things are dependent on a force or principle distinct from purely chemical or physical forces, allowing for the existence, at least by omission, of a Consciousness and of a soul. But Providence ordained the scientific revolution to occur in societies where Christianity thrived, forcing them *volens nolens* to adapt. Not all the islands of resistance have vanished; far from it. There is a wide range of situations between the progressivism of certain Protestant churches and the conservatism of Orthodox ones. But overall, in the course of their long evolution, Christians have learned to read the Bible differently, and even to subject it to the same methodological standards as the human sciences, such as history and literary criticism. Nothing suggests that theology has lost anything as a result or that the content of Scriptures has become any less important for believers.

Islam followed a very different path: a revelation, a radically different early expansion and an extraordinary golden age — but before the scientific revolution. With the Ottoman Empire's slow decline in the late 19th century and collapse after the First World War, Islam found itself increasingly relegated to the periphery of history, enduring events one after the other. Everywhere in the Muslim world, where populations are by and large poorly educated, a sort of latent war has been going on between ancients and moderns. The ancients draw strength from religion, practised in its most conservative forms given the context, while the modern find inspiration in Western Europe or, during the Cold War period, in the Soviet Union. Aside from the Shiite Iranian Revolution, it is only since the fall of communism that awareness of political Islamism has grown. Previously, it was present but inconspicuous. Islamist terrorism, the extremely perverse form of strategies of the weak against the strong, has become increasingly spectacular and widespread since 11 September 2001. Today, the weak have an edge because all of the resources of modern technology are at their disposal.

Considering that Sunni Islam is institutionally characterised by a total lack of centralisation, similarly to Protestantism, it is easy to understand why, unlike Christianity, Islam as a whole has not yet encountered the circumstances that would allow it to adapt to modernity. Its conservatism is manifested at a strictly religious level, but also in its attitude towards science and mores. With regard to the latter, Christian churches have gradually had to resign themselves to being more tolerant. It is also easy to grasp how a majority of Muslims, gripped with fear, are held captive by the trap of Islamist terrorism. However, as an outside observer, I fail to see why Islam would not be able to adapt in the long term, just as Christianity did over the centuries. but that will undoubtedly take several generations, despite the acceleration of history.

The previous paragraphs focused on the so-called "religions of the book" but I would like to quickly mention Buddhism, given its great importance in today's world. The following remarks also largely apply to Hinduism, of which Buddhism is an offshoot. Buddhism's main appeal lies in its focus on fostering the practical conditions for seeking earthly happiness, even in death. In that respect, it is a body of wisdom, accompanied by useful practices for personal development. On the metaphysical level, surprisingly, its vision of symbiosis between Mankind and the Cosmos, although very old on the scale of historical time, has not been shaken by physics' most revolutionary theories, unlike the religions "of the book" that are rooted in anthropocentrism. In particular, the concepts of reincarnation and nirvana are not incompatible with the theory of evolution's time scale or even the boldest space-time abstractions of physics. Moreover, the origins of Buddhism have, at least to a certain extent, protected it from the temptation of mixing religion and politics. It is very compatible with other Chinese spiritual traditions, such as Taoism or Confucianism, which are more guidelines for action.

Everything is naturally a matter of degree. In Burma, monasteries have a key place in society. Under the aegis of a leader as political as the Dalai Lama Tenzin Gyatso, Buddhism has been the vector of Tibetan nationalism and resistance to Tibet's full and total incorporation into the People's Republic of China in 1950. As for Hinduism, the stereotypical image of non-violence still conveyed by the memory of Mahatma Gandhi, who certainly was a "great soul" (the meaning of the word Mahatma), but also a politician and an eminent strategist, must be nuanced. In the context of India's struggle for independence, passive resistance was strategically the safest and smartest path. But ever since the subcontinent's partition in tragic conditions in 1947, religious violence has sporadically broken out in India, which remained a large Muslim country. Hinduism, which increasingly takes overtly nationalist or fundamentalist forms, bears a share of the responsibility for that. It is no coincidence if this part, like the previous one, ends with religion. It will remain present, though only in the background of the following part, which focuses on geopolitics.

III
THE SHOCK OF THE PRESENT

Geopolitics and international politics

From man's point of view, on every scale, the present is the grey area where the past and future overlap. The historian's task is not just to identify and connect certain aspects of the past's successive presents, but also to characterise remnants of the past in each present. Living with the times means reflecting or acting on the present. Ours is stuck between a very grim past, as seen in the previous part, and a future that looks very different from anything humanity has ever known, as demonstrated in previous chapters. The present has never experienced such a momentous tectonic shift, whose effects are felt in all our ways of understanding the world, in particular geopolitics, to which we will now turn a critical eye.

Until the early 1980s, theorists and practitioners in international relations banished that word from their vocabularies because of its negative association with past Germany. But it gradually came back into favour during that decade, and now there is a tendency to use it as a synonym for international politics everywhere. However, a careful distinction should be made between the two concepts. Using them interchangeably is a source of serious confusion that has grave effects on the power game among great nations.[1] The word geopolitics should only be used in reference to *ideology relating to territory*. The concept of ideology, which encompasses interpretations of history and culture, is wider than that of international relations. Unlike so many prophecies, globalisation has not abolished the relationship between populations and territories, which is rooted in history and geography. After a period of around two decades when the extension of production chains to a growing number of states seemed limitless, as though the whole Earth had already become a homogeneous theatre of operations — a field, as Bourdieu would have said — for companies of all nationalities, the general trend is now moving towards the relocalisation of industrial activities. If only in that regard, candidate Trump's position during the 2016 electoral campaign encouraged "sovereignists" in countries with less of a reputation for economic liberalism than the United States to uninhibitedly speak their minds.

Today, as in the past, major conflicts stem from the incompatibility between geopolitical projects, which always include

---

[1] See Thierry de Montbrial, *Action and Reaction in the World System*, UBC Press, Vancouver, 2013.

relatively visible identity dimensions. It should be stressed here that political leaders seldom explicitly spell out geopolitical projects and the ensuing "grand strategies", which are revealed more indirectly than directly. They need to be thoroughly analysed in order to be explained. Unlike many writers or observers, I think that the idea of power has lost none of its relevance in the 21st century and continues to play a pivotal role in the reality of international relations. But power is always connected to territory.[2] Geopolitics matters because, in conjunction with other ideologies, themselves based on the territory and identity (such as the universality of "Western values") that are more or less connected to them, it is the basis of international politics. Ideology is like a metalanguage that implicitly commands "grand strategies" when they exist, and more generally, the rationalisation of leaders' concrete choices.

International politics is the main activity of diplomats and servicemen, in theory under their governments' leadership. It involves states but also non-state political units. Confusing geopolitics and international politics makes it harder to thoroughly understand the present international system's structural instability and the vital need to improve global governance, the latter that necessarily requires a partial reappropriation of territories by citizens. For those worried about the risk of a Third World War, the crucial issue is that of global governance. A legitimate, effective framework for cooperation between states is indispensable.

---

[2] See "Qu'est-ce qu'une puissance au XXIe siècle" in Thierry de Montbrial, *La Pensée et l'action*, op. cit. or the website of the Académie des Sciences morales et politiques https://www.asmp.fr/travaux/communications/2013_01_07_demontbrial.htm.

The goal is to keep the world reasonably open and geopolitical inconsistencies from degenerating into major conflicts.[3]

Can it be said that governance made progress in the 20th century? To see more clearly, it is necessary to go back a century to the shock of the First World War, whose course and consequences nobody had foreseen. The myth of the "international community" began with the idea of collective security and the creation of an institution to promote it, the League of Nations. It was bound to fail after the United States' withdrawal from the League, even though it had been created at its initiative, and by its later indifference to the rise of fascism in Europe and Asia, and therefore to the march towards the Second World War. The winners of the Great War undoubtedly lost peace.[4] What interests us here is the global standpoint, of which there are three lessons to be drawn from the interwar period, whose relevance was confirmed over time.

The first is the importance of the relationship between economics and politics: fascism fed on the Great Depression. After clearing many hurdles, that lesson was partially taken into account from 1944 onwards, with the creation of institutions such as the International Monetary Fund, the World Bank or the GATT[5], which became the World Trade Organisation (WTO) in 1995. But later, they had trouble adapting, as was observed during the

---

3 See "La géopolitique entre guerre et paix" in Thierry de Montbrial, *La pensée et l'action*, *op. cit.* or http://www.thierrydemontbrial.com/wp-content/uploads/2009/05/X_FinalLesson.pdf.
4 See G.-H. Soutou, *La grande Illusion. Quand la France perdait la paix*, Paris, Tallandier, 2015.
5 General Agreement on Tariffs and Trade.

2007 "subprime crisis". Today's greatest threat is the protectionist temptation, in the broad sense of the term, which stems from the difficulty of adjusting to the digital civilisation, manifested in shifting combinations of unemployment and inequality. I will return to certain aspects of this issue later.

The second lesson is that no *community* worthy of the name can be based solely on a legal construction, especially in the absence of a binding framework. This is not to downplay the importance of the UN Charter, its derivatives and its successive enrichments — the embryo of an international criminal justice system or, in a different vein, the campaign against global warming. By and large, the WTO is doing remarkable work. States often seek international legality as a source of external and internal legitimacy. But reality compels us to acknowledge that law alone cannot settle the deepest geopolitical conflicts. Here are four very different examples: the Israeli-Palestinian question, Ukraine, Western Sahara and the islands in the East and South China Seas. Anybody who bothers to seriously study these conflicts before passing judgement on them understands that the players directly involved are willing to make tremendous sacrifices. They reject solutions imposed on them from the outside that are at odds with their interests, as defined by their geopolitical outlook in the broad sense. Long is the list of actions that conflict with international law. La Fontaine's famous verse, *Thus human courts acquit the strong, and doom the weak, as therefore wrong* (*The Animals Sick of the Plague*), has a universal reach. There is a double standard.

Nonetheless, for many states, even outside any ideology, the reference to the primacy of international law can be an elegant way to avoid taking a position on embarrassing situations, even if they seldom go so far as to condemn their allies that do not respect it. The conflicts in Eastern Europe, the Middle East or the islands claimed by China constantly offer examples.

The founders of the "European community" that started taking shape after the 1957 Rome treaties understood that real communities are based on a shared desire, nurtured in the long term, to increase the number of organic connections, and not just on a formal system of mechanical links such as international law. Today's organisation, renamed the "European Union" in 1992, actually undermines this conception of community. As this very Union shows cracks of weakness, how can anybody seriously speak of an "international community"? This is more than a matter of semantics. Used as often as the word "geopolitics", the expression conveys the wrong-headed belief that peoples, nations and states — each with their own characters — are no longer actors of history in today's world, an ideological and in reality often hypocritical position that is certainly easier to espouse at dinner parties in the West's great capitals than in formerly Communist countries or what was once called the "Third World". The ideology of the "international community" is explained by the Cold War, whose outcome gave Westerners the illusion that they shared a genuine geopolitical project that the rest of the world would spontaneously embrace. The United States held that belief at the time of the

1989 Tiananmen Square massacre or when they decided to topple Saddam Hussein in 2003. More generally, Western countries have too often believed that overthrowing a dictator — who they themselves had often put into power and supported, but that is another story — would suffice to usher in the best of all possible worlds. That pseudo-Leibnizian vision of history could inspire a new Candide.

If the question is, "Is it in the world's interest to come together as a community?", in my opinion the answer is yes in the very long term, no doubt far longer than a century. But that is still an abstraction. The question of building good global governance within one or two generations remains open.

The third lesson that can be learned from the failures of the interwar period is that the concepts of collective security and the balance of power are not mutually exclusive but are complementary.[6] American and Soviet leaders demonstrated that after the 1962 Cuban missile crisis, when cooperation (arms control, confidence-building measures, etc.) emerged from the shadow of nuclear dissuasion. To varying degrees depending on the place, the world has never stopped being "Westphalian". I will take that line of reasoning further by saying that the United Nations improved the League of Nations by including a Westphalian principle: the five permanent members of the Security Council with their veto power. I would add that no structural stability is possible without forms of balance between

---

6 Thierry de Montbrial, *Mémoire du temps présent, op.cit.*

the parties, even within a community worthy of the name. That also goes for the construction of Europe. Only the powerful can afford the illusion — or cynicism — of thinking that the idea of balance is outdated.

The following pages will examine certain features of recent trends on the international scene by looking at six complementary points of view: the primacy of the United States; the rise of China and, more generally, Asia; the difficulty of global economic governance; the missed opportunities after the end of the Cold War; the crisis of European construction; and the structure of the international system as a whole.

The primacy of the United States

The United States has kept its primacy for several reasons, only two of which I will discuss here. The first is that, in a world of weak or broken identities, theirs remains strong, despite racial tensions or the growth of social inequality. The United States is a land of immigrants that swept the plate clean, or almost, of its indigenous populations. From the outset, Americans have been bound together by a sacred text, the Constitution, which has survived more than two centuries of adventures and crises. The most recent is Trump's victory after an election campaign unlike any other, marked by a form of populism, in particular the rejection of traditional political elites. But Trump also represents the American Dream. With his slogan "Make America great again" and his desire to serve the national interest according to a right-wing gospel, he is in tune with his country, despite rubbing many of his compatriots the wrong way. The political and media elites, and the population as a whole, still have an unshakeable faith in the country's institutions. Any president who does not respect them would be voted out of office. That issue has many ramifications. For example, even if the 45th President intends to stop Mexicans from illegally crossing the border, the United States will remain a land of immigration — but within a rigorous framework, starting with the immigrants' commitment to obey American law as it derives from the Constitution. That has nothing to do with, for example, French-style ideological liberalism in favour of unconditional "diversity". The Constitution's role as the cornerstone of the United States' identity cannot be overemphasised. If an active minority transgressed it one day, there would be reason to start seriously worrying about the identity and therefore the future of the country. That day has not yet come.

The second reason for the primacy of the United States that I would like to underscore is the outstandingly effective "grand strategy" of means based on a simple idea: in all circumstances, the United States' armed forces must be bigger than any imaginable foreign coalition, beyond the allies or adversaries of the moment. As a result, related arms industries and, more generally, high-tech activities have been given top priority. But there is more. Rather well protected by their geography, Americans have always aimed for energy independence and increasingly overt domination in the area of information. Technology has allowed them to achieve both goals, in particular imposing themselves in the latter field. The only possible challenger in the foreseeable future is China, which is trying to catch up. The acronym GAFA sums up the situation well: search engines (Google), mobility (Apple), social media (Facebook) and e-commerce (Amazon), not to mention Microsoft. The singular combination of an unparalleled entrepreneurial culture and the active support of the government has enabled the United States, or rather California, to become the undisputed champion of big data, the Internet and innovation. No country, not even China, can hope to overtake it anytime soon. The United States has the whole world under surveillance and, militarily, can strike any target on the planet without running much risk — except, perhaps in the extreme event of war with other nuclear powers. It is easy to understand, then, how the United States would benefit if nuclear weapons were totally banned: it would no longer have anyone to fear, hence the regular campaigns in that direction.

America dominates the digital civilisation, still embryonic but bound to spread at a brisk pace. It is powerful enough to afford to make mistakes that the rest of the world cannot. It is not immune to cyberattacks, unpleasant revelations such as from Wikileaks, disinformation campaigns (whether or not they are called post-truth) or other attempts at destabilisation. But the United States durably — which does not mean eternally — seems like the best-prepared country in the world to overcome them.

And yet, the United States is in no position to govern the world. First of all, that is not part of its ideology and, even if it were, the country has often changed course in its history.

Protecting its territory and national identity, furthering its economic interests from a position of strength, making and unmaking alliances accordingly, reserving the sovereign right to strike abroad without fearing a counterstrike, and fostering the spread of its values to boost its soft power are the implicit, unchanging foundations of its foreign policy. This makes it less volatile in the long term than it seems to be in the short or medium term, and always reflects a unique, pragmatic combination where interests and values dovetail.

Certainties and uncertainties regarding China's rise

The starting point of contemporary China's emergence can be dated back to the late 1970s with the fall of the "Gang of Four", the end of the Cultural Revolution, the death of Mao Zedong and Deng Xiaoping's rise to real power. Of course, Japan preceded it with a success that lasted until 1990. The 1980s also saw the success of the "tigers", as South Korea, Taiwan, Singapore and Hong Kong were called then. The Chinese diaspora played a key role in the success of Deng's and his successors' reforms. In the early 1990s, India also started taking off by turning its back on the dogmatic socialism of the immediate post-independence period. The list could go on. But China's rise is what continues to mark global geopolitics as a whole, a situation recalling Prussia's ascension in 19th century Europe. Bismarck and Deng have something in common: the will to reform with clear ideas and from a position of strength — the exact opposite of Gorbachev at the end of the Soviet Union, weak and lacking vision. After the decompression of the "Crazy Years" decade, the brutal Tiananmen Square massacre in June 1989 shocked the world, but also made the West aware that, despite students celebrating the Statue of Liberty, millennia-old China was neither ready to throw itself into the arms of the United States nor to embrace Enlightenment ideology.

The great achievement of the governments that have followed one another in Beijing has been to preserve the legitimacy and authority of the Chinese Communist Party (CCP) while ensuring nearly four decades of unprecedented economic growth, cautiously but increasingly firmly asserting quasi-imperial national interests, opening up to the world and learning not only to participate in the bodies of global governance but also contributing to them with matchless skill by setting up institutions such as the Asian Infrastructure Investment Bank. The result, 40 years after The Great Helmsman's death, is that China, which still calls itself a People's Republic, ranks second in a global economy that has become very integrated, a situation in which they have so far been one of the main beneficiaries, as attested by Xi Jinping's speech at Davos in January 2017.

Meanwhile, China's rise has created some level of apprehension among its neighbours and, understandably, in the United States, which fears losing its superiority in the course of the 21st century. Hence, parallel to partially cooperative economic diplomacy,

Washington is implementing a sweeping containment policy that carries with it a serious risk of friction, especially in the South China Sea, where accidents leading to crises can be expected to occur. Nevertheless, the situation is very different from the Cold War. It is a chess game reminiscent of the 19th century and its "Westphalian" system, more than of the myth of an "international community" governed by law.

I mentioned the risk of accidents. The most important one in the short-medium term comes from North Korea, where even China's leaders seem incapable of reining in Kim Jong-un's uncontrollable behaviour. Their Confucian caution and competence, and the well-understood interests of the other players directly concerned (South Korea, Japan, Russia and the United States), undoubtedly reduce those risks, despite Trump's impulsiveness. But they are serious. That said, perhaps the most critical long-term challenge is inside China, where the harmonious pursuit of growth has come up against considerable stumbling blocks, including corruption, inequality, mass migration and environmental damage. Increasingly difficult reforms are necessary. Granted, the Chinese have a more reverential attitude towards their leaders than Europeans or Americans, but in the long term, the CCP's legitimacy depends on the pursuit of equitable growth. China's history is strewn with painful dynastic transitions. Contemporary China is no longer just a "Middle Empire" impervious to outside events. It is not immune to the challenges of the digital revolution or, more generally, the riptides rocking liberal societies and undermining authority. That explains why Xi Jinping's grip on power has been so strong after Hu Jintao's presidency, which was considered lax. But how sustainable is that policy? Not even China's leaders know for sure. However, it is clear that in the short and medium term, the need to contribute to the structural stability of the international environment as a whole as much as possible limits their tremendously ambitious grand strategy, which is rooted in a perfectly coherent geopolitical outlook (supremacy on the adjacent seas, the Silk Road, access to raw materials, etc.).

The difficult governance of the global economy

The upheavals brought about by the digital civilisation and unbridled offshoring from the 1980s on have made economic governance much more complex. Some of the classic issues of international trade, such as dumping or counterfeiting, remain relevant, but the rising number of offshore production chains has changed the nature and logic of the relationships between exports and imports. New challenges such as e-commerce are appearing. In addition to the growing complexity of trade (goods and services) and its effects on employment, migratory movements and the dissemination of investments, which have never been subjected to any multilateral framework, are reshuffling the international division of labour. The number of conflicts is rising, for example between the United States and Mexico over Trump's wall, or potentially between the European Union and China over the takeover of companies in liberal democracies by sovereign funds or public companies in illiberal countries. Multilateral trade has never been under so much threat since the Bretton Woods institutions were founded. China is now their strongest defender — a position that is only seemingly paradoxical, considering the asymmetrical advantages it has drawn from them for its own development. Whether in the area of international trade, migratory flows or the movements of capital, states will need to reassert themselves and strengthen cooperation with each other and with associations of states in order to avert a chaotic breakdown of the trade system and the return of suicidal forms of protectionism.

Despite the subprime crisis and the looming threat of another Great Depression, the coordination of macroeconomic policies has constantly conflicted with powerful states' desire to preserve their budgetary and fiscal autonomy, even within the Eurozone. As soon as he moved into the White House, Trump started dismantling the regulations the Obama administration had implemented in order to limit systemic risks. In contrast, central banks have never fully called into question their tradition of cooperation. They have not forgotten the consequences of the 1930s currency wars and launched unprecedented "non-conventional" policies in the wake of the subprime crisis in the late 2000s. But their capacity for action has come up against the lack of coherent government budget and tax policies. This is all the more true in highly economically integrated regions like the Eurozone, where resistance to shocks depends on the serious coordination of structural economic policies, which have largely failed. That is one of the main challenges facing Emmanuel Macron during his time in office.

The 2007 crisis and its aftermath tarnished some of the economists' lustre. The days when it was thought that economics would reach a degree of perfection comparable to the laws of classic mechanics seem to have receded into the distant past. Dating back to the 1960s, that belief undoubtedly explains why a Nobel Prize for Economics was created. The first was awarded in 1969. Speaking before the American Economic Association in 2003, the 1995 Laureate, Robert Lucas, proclaimed not the end of history, but of macroeconomics. *The central problem of depression-prevention has been solved*, he said four years before Lehman Brothers went bankrupt.[1] Not only was he wrong, but the mechanisms set up after the downturn triggered by the subprime crisis remain weak and willingness to cooperate always tends to evaporate when the perception of immediate danger recedes.

In conclusion, uncertainty has prompted signs of a resurgence of economic nationalism, even though interdependence is a reality, one which is impossible to roll back without major peril

---

1 See Avner Offer and Gabriel Söderberg, *The Nobel Factor. The Prize in Economics, Social Democracy, and the Market Turn*, Princeton University Press, 2016, p. 35, and Thierry de Montbrial, *La pensée et l'action, op. cit.*, p. 818.

on the planetary scale. That is why the short-term improvement of global governance, in other words within a generation, requires harmonising two movements: one towards the partial reconquest by states of their territories, the other towards closer and more demanding coordination of their policies.

The end of the Cold War: a missed opportunity

I now turn to a subject — the whole Eurasian continent, from the Atlantic coast to the Russian and Asian spaces east of the Urals and the Chinese sphere — that, historically, has always been at the heart of geopolitics.[1] To understand the present situation, it is necessary to return to the fall of the Soviet Union (USSR) in 1991, when the Russian Empire and the Communist system collapsed at the same time. The former lasted over two centuries, the latter three generations. For excellent reasons, the 20th century is often called the "Soviet century". We can hardly be surprised that such an earth-shattering event would continue to affect the geopolitical outlook of every player on the planet.

An analysis of the botched end of the Cold War perfectly

---

1 On the relationship between geopolitics and regional blocks, see Thierry de Montbrial, *Géographie politique*, PUF, "Que-Sais-je?" collection, 2006.

illustrates the difference between geopolitics as defined above and international politics as expressed in the more or less haphazard day-to-day march of events. It also sheds light on the naivety (or hypocrisy) of those who think that arbitration or law alone can settle major international conflicts.

It all started with two mistakes in the 1990s. Let us begin with Russia. In those years, when a whole spiritual and material world fell apart, "Europhiles", unlike "Slavophiles", sincerely thought that it would be possible to achieve a harmonious, durable *rapprochement* with the "West", or in practical terms, the Euro-Atlantic institutions: the European Community, which became the European Union with the Maastricht Treaty, and NATO. Incidentally, in American eyes, they are complementary international institutions like any other. The colourful Boris Yeltsin, who defeated Gorbachev, cultivated warm ties between the Kremlin and the West, even consulting American economic advisors and politicians. They even helped him win re-election in 1996, when the goal was to prevent the communist candidate, Zyuganov, from winning.[2] The comparison with Deng Xiaoping's China is very enlightening here. The Chinese too called on Western advisors, but only in the area of economics and merely as a useful source of inspiration, not necessarily to implement their ideas.[3] As the Russian President's family and friends became

---
2 See T. J. Colton, *Yeltsin. A Life*, New York, Basic Books, 2008.
3 See Julian Gewirtz, *Unlikely Partners: Chinese Reformers, Western Economists, and the Making of Global China*, Harvard University Press, 2017.

rich and oligarchs got their hands on the national wealth, the overwhelming majority of the population was struggling to survive. The number of warning signs pointing to a further break-up of the Russian Federation increased. People openly wondered whether it would completely fall apart and imagined the return of some sort of Grand Duchy of Moscow.[4] No wonder the Russians later considered the agreements concluded with the West in those years leonine. By the late 1990s, the whole country was awaiting a strongman to restore the country's unity and dignity. At the time, his name was still unknown: Vladimir Putin, who was appointed prime minister in 1999 and elected president in 2000.

Russia's present geopolitical outlook cannot be understood without recalling how it experienced the fall of the Soviet Union. In the 2000s, the regime's priority, overwhelmingly backed by the population, was to restore authority over the Federation's territory and prevent it from breaking up any further. In that new context, of course, ties had to be strengthened with Russia's "near abroad". In concrete terms, that meant applying the equivalent of the United States' Monroe Doctrine. Both in the Russian imagination and in reality, one country, Ukraine, has a key place in that regard. At first, "Europeanists" considered closer ties between Ukraine and the Western countries possible and even desirable, as long as they did not pose a threat to Russia's security.

---

[4] The author of this essay wrote about this period. See Thierry de Montbrial, *Journal de Russie*, Editions du Rocher, 2012.

Meanwhile, the prevailing geopolitical project of Western countries was rather different: they immediately took for granted that, once freed from the yoke of communism, Russia and the "Newly Independent States" would immediately embrace liberal democracy and the market economy for the good of their liberated peoples with, of course, the winners of the Cold War present on the ground. It was thus considered evident that the West should extend its reach to Ukraine, as the country was said to hold a pivotal role for the future of the Eurasian continent.[5] This idea, backed by Polish-born American political scientist Zbigniew Brzezinski (1928-2017),[6] gradually gained ground. Unsurprisingly, it benefited from the strong support of Poland and Lithuania — two of the countries that have suffered the most at Russia's hands during the course of their history — which joined the European Union at the same time. Ukraine, the rationale went, had to join the Union, and even more critically NATO, without delay and at whatever the cost. Ukraine's (as well as Georgia's) aspiration to join the Atlantic Alliance was asserted during the 2008 NATO summit's final declaration. The West considered it a natural right, Moscow a threat. Russia perceived the 2004 Orange Revolution in Kiev, portrayed in the West as spontaneous, as fomented by the United States. Convinced, since George W. Bush, that Washington had made regime change a

---

5 Z. Brzezinski, The Grand Chessboard, Basic Books, New York, 1997. Re-reading this work, some twenty years after it was first published, highlights more than ever the author's ideologies.

6 He was President Carter's national security advisor.

priority, and sensing imminent danger since the Maidan sit-in in late 2013, Putin decided to deter Ukraine from joining NATO after President Yanukovych's fall in 2014, which he saw as an echo of the Orange Revolution. The swift annexation of Crimea and the major geostrategic port of Sevastopol and interference in the Donbas followed. Putin must have been well aware of the long-term costs of his actions, but his current popularity is indicative that the overwhelming majority of Russians considered them necessary in the face of a vital threat.

With a bit of wisdom on both sides, Ukraine could have emerged as an area of cooperation benefitting all parties after the fall of the Soviet Union. Instead, it became the graveyard of East-West reconciliation. Worse, everything that had been patiently built up during the Cold War to prevent diverging geopolitical projects from igniting a Third World War (arms control, confidence-building measures, etc.) has been ruined. In a difficult global economic context, mistrust has spread to every issue, especially in the Near and Middle East, where different geopolitical and, more generally, ideological projects also clash: the overthrow of "undesirable" regimes, but without a clear vision of what happens next on the Western side, and support for authoritarian regimes and the balance of power on the Russian; and differing viewpoints on Islamist terrorism and how to counter it. Consequently, the Middle East and the fight against terrorism have suffered directly from the chilling of East-West relations — occurring against a backdrop of rivalries for influence rooted in history.

This is where we are at today. At least dialogue continues. The deterioration of East-West ties is not out of control, and the main parties involved have at least implicitly agreed to keep it that way. However, since the fall of the Soviet Union, no effort has been made to clearly identify areas of geopolitical friction, much less ways to reduce differences or at least means of peacefully coexisting with them while maintaining the ability to cooperate in areas such as the economy or the fight against terrorism, which would be immediately desirable for all parties. No sustainable diplomatic progress is possible without rising above the level of operational or tactical strategies. But is it conceivable, for example, that Trump and Putin may engage one day in such an in-depth conversation?

Unfortunately, even the European Union has been in deep crisis since 1989-1991. It has never seriously considered the need to clarify its members' geopolitical outlooks and bring them closer together, much less tried to overcome its problems with Russia. On the contrary, some member states seem to consider Russia their major threat. Yet Russia is aware of its limits and knows that its long-term future lies with the West, not China, with which it has had to draw closer out of necessity, though on China's terms. If Europe and Russia fail to find common ground in a reasonable lapse of time, both risk finding themselves reduced to being mere pawns in the great competition between the United States and China for domination of the Eurasian continent, which is already in full swing.

The European Union between peril and hope

From the standpoint of physical geography, Europe is the isthmus on which the Eurasian continent becomes the West. Its climate makes it very welcoming for humans. Its borders are conventionally defined by the Urals, the Caucasus and the Black Sea straits. From the demographic point of view, it attracts populations from the East and South. Roughly 100 million of Russia's official population of 146 million live in Europe on seven million square kilometres, the rest in Asia on 10 million square kilometres, an area bigger than China, which has 1.3 billion people. From the historical perspective, Europe is the cradle of science and modernity. Despite a relentless "civil war", it dominated the world until the plague of nationalism gave way to the First World War and led to a form of collective suicide. Since the Second World War, international politics has been marked by a faltering attempt to build a new type of political unit, whose intellectual roots reach back to the Age of Enlightenment (Abbé de Saint-Pierre, Kant), the necessity of which began to emerge between the wars.

Europe did not start coming together as a serious geopolitical project until the start of the Cold War, especially after the failure, in 1954, of the European Defence Community, which France wanted and then rejected. The Treaty of Rome, which marked the birth of the European Economic Community (EEC), was signed on 25 March 1957. Its unique institutional organisation attested of the novelty of its geopolitical project. In particular, the European Commission aimed to represent the interests of the Community as a whole. Each member was supposed to forget, so to speak, its country of origin. The EEC would probably not have seen the light of day without the Soviet threat then looming over Western Europe and the United States' commitment to it through the 1949 North Atlantic Treaty. But the necessary conditions were seldom sufficient and it took inspirational, energetic leaders, such as Jean Monnet and Robert Schuman in France, for the project to start taking shape, based on the foundation of Franco-German reconciliation, democracy and the market economy. The first two main steps with regard to the latter were the establishment of the Customs Union on 1 July 1968 and the European Monetary System (EMS) 10 years later. The original Community had six members, with France in the leading role: Germany and Italy had lost the war; Belgium, the Netherlands and Luxembourg were too small.

The European Union between peril and hope

For the founding fathers, the long-term goal was to create a sort of "United States of Europe" along the same lines as the United States of America, but they disagreed on the organisation's ultimate geographical boundaries. They either held to a precise but inevitably conventional, and therefore prone to conflicts, territorial perimeter; or acknowledged the possibility for an *a priori* limitless expansion. The first view was historical-geopolitical, the second, universalist. The issue has never been settled and, in my opinion, does not need to be. Time will tell, as it does for all human endeavours. In practice, the first major territorial debate involved the United Kingdom, which was interested in the Customs Union and, as always, eager to become enmeshed in continental politics. France's partners, which saw the United Kingdom as a counterweight to the *"grande nation"*, welcomed its bid, but General de Gaulle did not, arguing that London's geopolitical outlook was incompatible with the European project. Georges Pompidou, who succeeded him as president, was less keen on history and geography. He got along well with Edward Heath, a fervent European and his partner at 10 Downing Street. The decision was made to go forward with the first expansion of the Community, which grew from six to nine members, the United Kingdom bringing Ireland and Denmark in its wake. The dialectical relationship between widening and deepening concretely dominated the territorial debate until the fall of the Soviet Union. Each step had to be consolidated before taking the next. Greece joined on 1 January 1981, Spain and Portugal on 1

January 1986, Austria, Finland and Sweden on 1 January 1995. Valéry Giscard d'Estaing promoted Greece's membership after the fall of the military dictatorship in Athens. The admission of Spain and Portugal followed their democratisation after the deaths of Franco and Salazar. The increase from 12 to 15 member states, decided before the fall of communism, was bolder because the newcomers were neutral, each in its own way. Meanwhile, the main steps deepening the Community involved creating, under the impetus of Valéry Giscard d'Estaing and Helmut Schmidt, the European Monetary System, which resolved the chaos of national currencies; the election of the European Parliament by universal direct suffrage (10 June 1979), which Giscard and Schmidt also wanted; and initiatives such as the Erasmus programme (15 June 1987).

The 15-member European Union was still relatively viable, even though the founders' spirit was progressively drifting farther away and the practical operating difficulties of an increasingly cumbersome, bureaucratic institutional system. But the commitment of the "Franco-German couple" never wavered. The original geopolitical project of European construction would not have survived without it. The major turning point was the fall of the Soviet Union (1989-1991) and its first consequence: German reunification and the liberation of Central and Eastern Europe. This extraordinary and totally unpredictable event, at least in its details and above all in its timing, immediately sparked a debate on the European Community's future that had to be settled quickly.

To avoid the risk of chaos, the choice of a new wave of enlargement prevailed over the erection of a hypothetical confederation. On 2 May 2004, eight former communist states joined the Community (now the European Union): Poland, Hungary, the Czech Republic and Slovakia (the former Czechoslovakia); Estonia, Latvia and Lithuania (the three Baltic republics annexed by the USSR in 1940); and Slovenia, a remnant of the former Yugoslavia. Cyprus and Malta also became members at the same time and somewhat on the sly. Bulgaria and Romania joined three years later on 1 May 2007. The European Union thus had 27 members, and then 28 with the admission of Croatia, who like Slovenia was a remnant of the former Yugoslavia (1 May 2013). Several states of Southeastern Europe, starting with Serbia, knocked on Europe's door, not to mention Turkey, with which membership talks began in late 2005. The Balkan region has been at the crux of European politics since the weakening and disappearance of the Ottoman Empire. The issue was partially buried during the Cold War because of the East-West divide. Today the trend is towards integrating the Balkans and, therefore, internalising their problems within the European Union. Managing that integration is one of the Union's greatest challenges. In the two decades after the fall of communism, the ideology of enlargement at any cost has prevailed, even extending, as I showed above, to Ukraine — with no regard for the economic and political realities of the moment.

The most astounding thing is that the Community edifice is still standing after all those changes. It inspired so much hope! True to the spirit of the Union's founding, albeit in a throughouly different context and balance of power, France (François Mitterrand) and Germany (Helmut Kohl) first sought new ways to deepen the Union and adapt its institutions. The first stage climaxed with the Maastricht Treaty (7 February 1992) and entry into force of the Schengen Agreement (26 March 1995), the second with a treaty instantly considered flawed (the Treaty of Nice, signed 26 February 2001), soon replaced by the constitutional project. Maastricht led to the euro's creation and entry into force in 12 countries (1 January 2002), but France and the Netherlands rejected the European Constitution (May-June 2005). The Union fell back on a new treaty (Lisbon, 13 December 2007), which was much less legitimate. The Eurozone started off in a blaze of glory, despite its *de facto* guarantors' lack of budgetary discipline. Germany had the excuse of the cost of reunification, but Chancellor Schroeder had the courage to put his country's financial house in order. France did not, repeatedly setting a poor example. In the wake of the subprime financial crisis, which started in the United States (2007), the Eurozone's structural weaknesses started showing before crystallising, especially around Greece (the first bail-out plan was in May 2010). Meanwhile, the poorly managed "Arab Spring" crisis accelerated chaos in the Middle East and increased the flow of refugees, revealing flaws in the implementation of Schengen. At the same time, Islamist terrorism increased. The European Union's inability to deal with so many crises at once was plain to see. Loss of faith in its geopolitical project spread. People affected by the economic downturn blamed globalisation and Brussels, tarring both with the same brush. Some former communist countries refused to recognise the European institutions' right to limit their sovereignty, for example by imposing refugee quotas. When the British voted to leave the Union on 23 June 2016, the European project seemed to be on the verge of collapse. In that regard, it is time to question the system of holding referenda on issues affecting an entire people's long-term future. At the very least, the requirement of a qualified majority, or a simple majority confirmed by a second referendum after a reasonable amount of time, could be considered. Obviously, this remark does not apply to Great Britain alone.

One year later, the European storm has died down a bit. Brexit did not have the immediate effects that had been feared. States, such as the Netherlands or Hungary, that had began to flirt with the idea of leaving have decided to stay. Public opinion in every Eurozone country backs the single currency. That is one reason why Marine Le Pen lost the presidential election on 7 May 2017 by such a wide margin. Despite their unruly nature and attraction to eccentric characters like Jean-Luc Mélenchon, the French want to remain in the European Union. An overwhelming majority elected a candidate who clearly campaigned in favour of Europe and the euro and on the urgency of solving the country's structural problems. Emmanuel Macron wants to restore France and Germany's historic role in order to correct the European

Union's flaws and allow it to bounce back. The Fifth Republic's eighth president knows that putting the national economy back on a sound footing is a prerequisite for success. In that regard, the situation he inherits looks similar to the one in 1958, when General de Gaulle returned to power in the context of the Algerian War. In reality, France's economic recovery in 2017 will be harder than it was then because the problems are more structural. Nevertheless, Macron's election aroused worldwide interest, revealing muffled hopes for Europe, and consequently, for France because of its position as a key player. It is these expectations of Europe that must now be understood.

First, let us dispel the idea that Europe is in a state of decay. Of course, the European civil war and the rise of the United States dominated the first half of the 20th century. But despite all its flaws, the considerable achievements in the decades after the Second World War — reconstruction, economic and social development, decolonisation, the beginning of European construction, and the expansion of democracy — were a veritable renaissance. In its post-Brexit configuration, the European Union is a developed and already relatively integrated whole with a population of around 450 million. Combined, France and Germany alone are much more demographically and economically powerful than Japan. If, in the medium term, the Union can ensure its security better, fight Islamist terrorism, organise immigration, manage the refugee problem and increase its education and social protection systems' effectiveness, it may shine more brightly than ever. Despite lagging behind in the field of digital technology, it still has considerable potential and its rich cultural heritage remains equal to none in the world. If European construction attracts a seemingly disproportionate amount of the world's attention, it is also for geopolitical reasons. In East Asia for example, states like Japan or South Korea no longer hide their anxiety about relying almost completely on the United States for their security. They no longer hesitate to show their long-term interest in a stronger European Union, not just economically and socially, but also in security and defence matters. For these same crucial reasons, and inadvertently spurred on by Trump, the Union is finally considering taking its security into its own hands, starting with all the aspects relating to Islamist terrorism. Immunised by past excesses, the outside world no longer perceives it as an imperialist threat, provided it resists the temptation of "human-rightist" propaganda, as Hubert Védrine would say. It can develop new kinds of partnerships with its neighbours, starting with Great Britain, once the divorce is settled, and certainly with Turkey. In cooperation with others, such as Japan, it could also contribute more to the development and stabilisation of Africa, now vulnerable to covetousness from around the world. Latin America also has a place in those kinds of considerations, which makes the geopolitical project of European construction even more ambitious.

It seems to me that the project's appeal also, and essentially, lies in that it is a kind of a laboratory where a new type of political unit is being experimented. The vision of the United States of

Europe is naïve if it implies imitating the American model, which holds radically different historical roots. But it can make sense with the strengthening of existing organic links; better managed and respectful of member states' diversity and cultures. In the Union as it exists, those links already go far beyond inter-state relations or international law. That is the fundamental reason why the Community, which the Maastricht Treaty renamed a Union, has survived the tremendous shock of the Soviet Union's disappearance and the admission of new members that immediately followed. Returning to the issue of territorial limits, it can be said that they are not predetermined. In every period, they are the furthest boundaries possible without threatening the whole edifice with collapse. Naturally, whenever the Union expands, the newcomers put their stamp on the old members and vice versa. In one or two centuries, or perhaps more, it might be possible to speculate on the good global governance of a world that will have become even more interdependent than it is now, if only because of technology's relentless progress. The development of such governance could benefit from the European experience, with its successes and failures. One day, European construction might even be seen as a key step on the way towards the creation of a political unit on the planetary scale.

The international system

The term *international system* conveniently expresses the idea that international society comprises interacting units: associations of states, states, regions, cities, international organisations, companies, non-governmental organisations, religious communities, criminal organisations, etc. Anyone who manages to fully and perfectly describe that system and its members' various ideologies, histories and projects might be able to foresee the outlines of its development, or at least significantly lower the degree of uncertainty about the future. They could also confidently draw up the guidelines for its governance, in other words the coordination methods necessary to achieve goals in the common interest, notably the peaceful settlement of certain major conflicts or the maintenance of major economic balances.

But possessing such knowledge is impossible. To the

uncertainty inherent in the evolution of any system (no matter how well analysed) is compounded the arduous uncertainty surrounding the system itself. That is why Valéry's pessimism about predictions in history still rings true today. Yet, despite the increasing levels of uncertainty, it is never total and degrees of relevance can be discerned in the countless possible discourses on the future. Otherwise, there would be no discernable reality. There would only be room left for a brutal clash of ideologies, which it is true many players or commentators nurture.

The following lines do not claim to present a complete, relevant discourse on the present international system, but merely hope to identify some of its key features to better guide us through the fog. I will mention four: heterogeneity, globality, multipolarity and complexity.

By *heterogeneity* I primarily mean that the international system's interacting units have very different natures, sizes and power. They must not be lumped together. In all the excitement over liberal globalisation after the fall of the Soviet Union, the prevailing discourse proclaimed the end of the state. The opposite happened. Since the new century began, states have reasserted their primacy and, consequently, the classic trilogy that characterises them according to law: a territory, a population and a government. The good governance of other active units, such as companies, is subordinate to inter-state cooperation, for example in legal or fiscal matters.

None of that should prevent us from recognising another

aspect of reality: the heterogeneity of states as such, whose identities, typically, can be more or less fractured. In the previous pages, it was pointed out that the identity of the United States remains remarkably strong, whereas that of France, for example, is fraying. But even with resources, a country whose identity is lastingly and seriously fractured would find it hard to conduct a strong foreign policy, because foreign policy is the concrete emanation of a geopolitical outlook closely connected to the sense of identity. There are also many quasi or failed states, especially in the Middle East and Africa, where governments do not control their territories, inevitably setting the stage for external conflicts that cannot remain contained unless other states cooperate with them in order to reach that goal. That takes us back to the issue of governance. The case of a failed state is extreme, for there are countries, even in Europe, such as Great Britain, Belgium and France, with pockets of territory *de facto* outside government control, which, in the short term, foster terrorism. Countries that allow such situations to last do so at their peril. The case of states with tribal traditions is also worth mentioning, especially in the Middle East and Africa, where the exercise of governmental authority is inherently limited by the power of tribal leaders, which often straddles several states. The result can be major difficulties on the international level, for example when Saudi Arabia or Qatar were accused of funding terrorism.

But heterogeneity has another, equally as thorny aspect. Because each state has its history, it also has one or more identity and geopolitical discourses, more or less competing, but usually with a leitmotiv. The exponents of "liberal globalisation" made the ideological mistake of believing in the immediate dawn of an international community governed by the economy and companies for the benefit of the general welfare. That ideology is fading away. But the word "liberal" has several different meanings and there is at least one other way to interpret the expression "liberal globalisation": a universal community of states sharing the main features of Western political ideology. As we have seen, after the fall of communism, the triumphant West hastened, if not caused, the fall of rogue regimes. All ideologies eventually come up against reality and spawn counter-ideologies, and this case was no exception. We witnessed the rise of illiberal forces, even within the European Union, where they have won elections in at least two states: Hungary and Poland. The case of President Erdogan's Turkey is especially striking given its NATO membership and its key position at the crossroads of Europe, Asia and the Middle East. By conspicuously turning his back on "Western values", and therefore on Kemalism, backed by a slim majority of the population, Erdogan — and he is not alone — shows that, despite the West's confidence in the superiority of its values, the future is not European. And indeed, a glance at the map of the Eurasian continent suffices to realise that history is not currently moving in this direction.

The West thus faces a choice: to acknowledge and accept this heterogeneity, refraining from all value judgements and focusing its efforts on seeking mutually beneficial forms of cooperation with a view to keeping the world reasonably open and viable; or to oppose it more or less head-on, accepting the risk of ideological escalation and so, at the very least, of the possibility of a new Cold War with redrawn geographical boundaries. The question thus posed is truly geopolitical, in the precise sense I have given the term, and it has evidently not been clearly settled yet. In international politics, it has prompted sub-questions, such as what attitude to take towards authoritarian or dictatorial regimes, especially in the Middle East, and not just that of Bashar al-Assad in Syria.

Globality, naturally, is a phenomenon of globalisation whose fundamental cause is a scientific and technological revolution, unprecedented in the history of humanity, as I have repeated several times in this essay. It has already produced considerable effects, but the most important ones are yet to come. It affects the international system and therefore, the uncertainty that surrounds it, in many ways. As a result, the diversity and identity of the active units forming the system are being modified, concurrently to their resources and their ability to use them. That goes first and foremost for states. In particular, economic structures are bound to change in every country on the planet, with varying ideological and political effects depending, in large part, on the identity and therefore, the history of each nation. As we have seen, technology as such does not automatically lead to the delocalisation of production chains. On the contrary, there are good reasons to believe that the relocalisation trend in some countries might last. But localisation is just one aspect of adaptation and the most conservative states have little chance of ranking among the winners.

Technology, then, changes not only all of the active units and their structure upon which the international system is based, but also, and perhaps especially, the network of links connecting them, which are both more numerous and correlated. Even if states or associations of states, temporary or lasting such as the European Union, learn to better regulate the tangible or virtual flows likely to affect their security in the broad sense of the term (including flows of capital, migrants or refugees), none can expect to be completely safe from information of all kinds streamed by omnipresent technology. What historians call the movement of ideas has always been a key factor of change, as the Enlightenment in 18th century Europe and the series of revolutions that followed illustrate. And at the time, information travelled slowly and only in certain directions. Today, it moves instantaneously and in theory universally. Even in China, skirting Internet censorship is easy. It is hard to assess the impact of that key aspect of globalisation. The behaviour of states has not changed with Wikileaks, with the increase of disinformation and rumours (renamed fake news), or with the accusations of Russian meddling in elections in liberal democracies. From an organisational perspective, technology can foster democracy or its opposite. It can help to develop personal life or destroy it. There would be much to say on this subject.

However, it is possible that, after a totally libertarian stage when public officials on every level were helpless in regulating the flow and content of information on the Internet, we have already begun to climb a learning curve likely to result in forms of regulation or control, with the gradual emergence of new laws straddling domestic and international law. If it is true, as I believe, that in today's world, peace based on law alone remains an elusive goal, law nevertheless remains more than ever a key instrument to prevent at all levels, the two extremes of dictatorship or anarchy and the ever-present risk that one will lead to the other. Thus, in the world to come, it is crucial to foster the emergence of law adapted to new forms of interdependence. That is a key and still developing aspect of future global governance.[1]

I will now turn to *multipolarity*. After the fall of the Soviet Union, the international system was called unipolar, multipolar, pluripolar or even apolar in turn. That terminological volatility reflects the objective difficulty of identifying it, as the system itself has fluctuated while keeping some permanent, or, if one prefers, invariable, features. Multipolarity is one of them, provided, as always, that the term is defined. What I mean by pole is any state with the goal of influencing how its neighbourhood is organised — inevitably through a geopolitical project, which can be more or less compatible with those of other states — and willing to lastingly commit resources to that end. However, faced with any

---

[1] See M. Delmas-Marty, *Aux quatre vents du monde. Petit guide de navigation sur l'océan de la mondialisation*, Seuil, 2016.

concrete situation, and therefore on the level of international politics, the effort depends on the dialectical relationship between interests and means in the circumstances of the moment. The neighbourhood can be more or less local or, in the example of the UN Security Council's five permanent members (the United States, Russia, China, France and the United Kingdom), span the planet. Others, such as India, generally considered a great power today, still limit themselves to their immediate neighbourhood. Resources are economic, diplomatic, military or cultural in various combinations and degrees.[2] That definition makes it easier to objectively name the poles, starting with the Security Council's permanent members; but also, and already, to a lesser extent, Japan, Germany and others on a regional level. I will not dwell on the difficulty of the idea of region in geopolitics.

That said, in the Middle East, for example, five states clearly qualify as regional poles: Turkey, Iran, Saudi Arabia, Egypt and Israel. Generally, as the Middle East shows, lasting peace in a region is impossible today without a *geopolitical agreement* between the regional poles and the outside poles most concerned, endorsed by the legitimacy and legality provided by the UN framework. With regard to the Middle East, the outside poles are the Security Council's five permanent members, some of which are more active than others, to which Germany must also be undoubtedly added. An agreement's longevity depends on how much coherence is achieved in adjusting different geopolitical outlooks to each other,

---

[2] See Joseph Nye's soft power.

given that they shift, usually slowly, with circumstances.

That also applies to the economy. In the absence of clear-cut membership guidelines, is the G20 an adequate list of international economic poles? Another question is that of its functioning. But how can it be more effective when economic cooperation is still so woefully inadequate within the European Union? Truth be told, the management of economic interdependence is still relatively embryonic.

Without claiming to rival the major powers, some regional poles can achieve a level of economic development and political maturity allowing them to contribute to the entire international system's structural stability. They can be called medium powers. South Korea, for example, aspires to become one. Common sense suggests that the world as a whole would have much to gain from the emergence of medium powers on every continent wanting to constructively cooperate on organising the future international system.

The UN's legitimacy also depends on regional organisations such as the Arab League or the African Union, which are still too few and too weak. Supplementing and strengthening them is an important goal for future global governance. That observation allows me to follow up with another key aspect of the international system: the distinction between the centre and the periphery. Put simply, any serious crisis in the system's core mechanically affects the whole, while the effects of a crisis on the periphery usually remain limited. The possibility of psychological or ideological interference justifies linguistic caution. Few events in Latin America are likely to have a noticeable, lasting impact on the whole planet. Chavez's dictatorship ruined Venezuela but the rest of the world hardly noticed. Likewise, most events in Africa so far have left the system's core unaffected.

Let us focus on Africa for a moment. Putting aside political correctness, it is always considered peripheral. Yet many African countries have made economic and even, although more timidly, political strides in the past 20 years. The continent has considerable natural resources, which great powers covet — not just the former European colonial powers, but also China, which was already present under Mao Zedong, and others. Since the early 2010s and the fall of the Gaddafi regime in Libya, the Sahel has drawn more attention from the centre due to both the growth of terrorist groups operating there and the swelling tide of African refugees arriving in Europe. That said, none of Africa's regional poles, not even South Africa or Nigeria, has yet sought to become a medium-size power in the sense defined above, or even to credibly portray itself as wanting to constructively participate in managing the international order as a whole. Africa's regional organisations remain weak. Some conflicts, such as the strife in the Western Sahara, stay latent and have become sources of fierce propaganda. Until the "Arab Spring", the African continent was undeniably situated at the periphery of the international system. Now, we know that it is not safe from the risk of major shocks, which are certainly unpredictable in detail, but hold global repercussions.

Paradoxically, *complexity* is a simple idea. A cause-and-effect relationship is complex when a small variation in the cause can be amplified in its effects so that, in a sort of chain reaction, the system eventually "explodes" in an unpredictable direction. That phenomenon, called "non-linearity", was popularised in the 1960s in meteorology with the name the "Butterfly Effect". A well-known example in economics is when a financial bubble bursts. The 2007 subprime crisis sent shock waves through the world's economy and nearly caused a crisis comparable to the Great Depression in the 1930s. Politically, the history of the "Arab Spring" perfectly illustrates the phenomenon: in 2010, a man sets himself on fire somewhere in the middle of Tunisia; Ben Ali's authoritarian regime collapses; civil war breaks out in Libya; Gaddafi is eliminated; Mubarak is overthrown in Egypt; parts of Syria rise up and the wildfire spreads across the Middle East.

Everything suggests that the proliferation of "non-linear" connections in the international system, continuously changing since the 1990s, has greatly increased risks of that kind, especially since those connections remain poorly understood. Many of them derive directly from technology, starting with social media, whose role during the "Arab Spring" has been well documented. They drive an uncontrollable intensification of emotions, and the slightest mistake by governments can spiral into a major uncontrollable crisis. But that can happen anywhere and, as I have already said, no state, as authoritarian and borderline dictatorial as it may be, can feel completely safe. Any crisis in a pole in the international system ripples through the whole system. Not even the most hotheaded advocates of changing the established order can brush aside that type of uncertainty. Generally, the history of revolutions shows that reform, as means of adaptation, is a better path.

The question, then, is this: can a system whose non-linearity might multiply the butterfly effect be regulated? With regard to the international system, the answer is no on two counts. First, as mentioned before, it is impossible to know the whole system in detail. Second, because even if it could be regulated, it would be impossible to react to all *a priori* small shocks under the pretext that they might spiral out of control into a catastrophe or a bifurcation. Thus, such an observation suggests that it is the system itself that must be changed by acting on its most fundamental features, which are the most identifiable. Strengthening a network of reasonably cooperative global and regional poles; encouraging the rise of medium-sized powers without agressive ideological preaching but with the shared goal of keeping the world tolerant and reasonably open; forging strong links not only in order to promote reforms in the common interest but also to react quickly in the event of a crisis; bolstering the framework of legitimacy, in other words the UN system as a whole, including its regional branches; and spurring the emergence of legal systems geared to the technological revolution, are the key markers of a global governance adapted to the coming times. Building it will inevitably take a very long time. By nature, it will never be finished. It will meet with resistance in big and small states alike. It can only be achieved by experimentation, trial and error. Today, nobody can claim to have a ready-made governance architecture or to know exactly where we stand. The present is exciting for those trying to live it to the fullest, but it is also perilous. Those who believe that the return of great catastrophes can be avoided by blowing up borders and overthrowing political regimes they dislike are mistaken. The negative has never been enough to create the positive. The future will not be built on the denial of reality and the abstraction of a Rousseau-like world. The many people responsible for global governance must think about it pragmatically and openly enough to allow the human spirit to continue producing, through the diversity of cultures and civilisations, the brightest prospects for humanity as a whole.

Epilogue

As the third decade of the 21st century approaches, our future is laden with uncertainty. It is heavy with unknown unknowns. In the United States, international relations specialists tend to reduce discussion to the outcome of the showdown between the United States and China, assuming that the vitality of the former does not lapse and that the latter continues to successfully overcome, i.e. without major domestic problems, the huge challenges that come with its development. In his last bestseller, drawing on case studies from universal history, Graham Allison describes as highly likely a new "Thucydides Trap": a collision between the rising power (in this case, China), and one possibly in the process of being defeated (the US). In 19th century Europe, the obvious parallel is the rise of Prussia and the three major conflicts that followed: the Franco-Prussian War of 1870, followed by the two world wars of the 20th century, which no one had foreseen before 1914. These tragedies led the US to oust Britain in its role as a *de facto* leader of the international system.

Casting off Allison's assumption, Joseph Nye sees the future being shaped by the "Kindelberger Trap," named after a US economist famous in his time, particularly for his analyses of the Great Depression of the 1930s, the political consequences of which are all-too-familiar to us. In Kindelberger's opinion, which is shared by many others, the root of evil was the bankruptcy of global governance at the time, when London had ceased to exercise its global responsibilities and was clumsily trying to go all or nothing, while Washington was still behaving like a free rider. Joseph Nye believes that the fundamental issue of present time, as it was during the interwar period, is that of global governance. That is also my firm belief, as I said at the outset in the foreword to this book.

The interdependence between the US and China has become such that neither of the two powers is currently looking for a direct face-off, even if both were to adopt the narrowest views of their national interests. Despite all their shortcomings, unlike Europe in 1870 or 1914, the UN system and the present functioning of state-to-state relations make a "war by accident" unlikely today. I see only a major misstep on Taiwan as a possible exception. However, the world today is characterised by a multitude of peripheral instabilities, both in the west and the east of the Eurasian continent. What's more, these instabilities are correlated.

However, thousands of years of experience suggest that the collision between these centres may be the result, more or less unpredictable in its detail, of peripheral disorders, when each of these centres, captive of a blinkered vision, seeks to exploit them at the expense of its rival.

In reality, interdependence today is a universal reality, and the destabilisation of societies due to the successive waves of the technological revolution can be seen everywhere. Concurrent to this, the spread of ideas, information, or misinformation has never been so intense and instantaneous. It is largely beyond states' power. Refugee displacements and migratory pressure have never been so lightly controlled, except for during times of major historical disaster. If the risk of a third world war became real, it would be the result of a chaotic degeneration of this global phenomenon. In the final phase of the Cold War (the real one, not the current artificial cold war between the Atlantic Alliance and the Russian Federation), the risk of a direct confrontation between the US and the Soviet Union had massively shrunk back into the shadows of nuclear deterrence and arms control, and competition between the two "superpowers" had moved — with a great deal of restraint — into what was then called the "Third World." However, the game has changed. Firstly, due to an event that no one could have foreseen, at least in terms of timing: the implosion of the continental superpower. I have never met anyone who seriously voiced the idea that the US or China might implode, say, in the next 20 years. Secondly and most importantly, the new Third World is infinitely more proteiform than the old one, and an unbridled Sino-American competition in this new Third World could take on the most dangerous turns.

Whatever the angle taken, we always come back to the need to strengthen global governance. Yet, despite so many forecasts in the opposite direction, it appears that the core of the international system has remained inter-state. Even weakened, states remain by far the leading players in this system. They have, admittedly, become fragile, to varying degrees; even the most powerful. The Western liberal democracies of the present day are not shining examples of "good government" capacity. Soft power, carried by the very idea of democracy, has taken a hit because of it. The most enlightened of illiberal democracies — those that do not recognise *individual freedom* as the ultimate value — are tightening up as they watch the swirl of more or less anarchic ideas from the outside rush in. Even the most successful models like the multi-ethnic city-state of Singapore can feel threatened. And some of the most authoritarian regimes are now fighting just to survive. In any case, the temptation for one party to cast the blame on others for all the difficulties it is experiencing at home is omnipresent, as can be seen every day in the many facets of populism or nationalism. In such a downgraded environment, while the US is only thinking about its narrowest interests and the notion of global leadership is foreign to Chinese thinking, the chances of an indispensable strengthening of international cooperation, and thus of global governance, appear at first glance very slim.

Epilogue

The primary mission of the embryonic global civil society formed by the planet's main think tanks is, in my opinion, to work toward a better understanding of the risk thus involved and, through their influence, to encourage the main states to become aware of a two-fold necessity. First, that they acknowledge the reality of the heterogeneous international system which I have described in this book; to recognise the need to cooperate in good faith within the bounds of mutually agreed playing rules, even if this implies adapting them regularly, punishing deviant and thus revolutionary states in a concerted way, but also helping such states fall back in line if they show goodwill. The response will be that this is the role of the UN, particularly the Security Council. While I do not underestimate the value of that organisation, in practice it cannot do much, if states continue to regard it as a theatre stage. It is the states themselves that write the play. Secondly, the main states need to explicitly contribute to the common good, by committing themselves to conceive their national interest in a sufficiently broad way so that this can happen. The problem is that none of this comes naturally. What I am saying probably does not echo with a Donald Trump or a Recep Tayyip Erdoğan. But even kings are not eternal and they can change. I think that a Xi Jinping or even a Vladimir Putin can hear something in these comments. As can many more. From this point of view, too, I feel it is essential that the efforts towards regional integration — starting with the European Union, but also ASEAN and other models — be continued, tirelessly. More generally, the medium-sized powers have a critical part to play in rescuing global governance, for their survival as players in history depends on it. It was, first and foremost, with them in mind that I wrote this book.

Thierry de Montbrial

www.ingramcontent.com/pod-product-compliance
Lightning Source LLC
Chambersburg PA
CBHW061942220426
43662CB00012B/1995